Nick Vandome and John S C McVey

Effective Communications

In easy steps is an imprint of In Easy Steps Limited
4 Chapel Court · 42 Holly Walk · Leamington Spa
Warwickshire · United Kingdom · CV32 4YS
www.ineasysteps.com

Notice of Liability
Every effort has been made to ensure that this book contains accurate
and current information. However, In Easy Steps Limited and the
author shall not be liable for any loss or damage suffered by readers
as a result of any information contained herein.

Trademarks
All trademarks are acknowledged as belonging to their respective
companies.

In Easy Steps Limited supports The Forest Stewardship Council (FSC),
the leading international forest certification organisation. All our titles
that are printed on Greenpeace approved FSC certified paper carry the
FSC logo.

MIX
Paper from
responsible sources
FSC® C020837

Printed and bound in the United Kingdom

ISBN 978-1-84078-448-0

Contents

1 Why Does it Have to be so Hard?

We all need communications in the workplace, to keep us informed and help us make decisions. This chapter introduces the corporate communications process and covers some of the areas that should be addressed when communicating at work.

The Art of Communications

On the surface, the world of corporate communications is a simple one: we all communicate, all of the time, so why should it be a problem?

But despite its apparent simplicity, successful communications is a skill like any other in the workplace and one that needs to be constantly worked at and developed. Most importantly, if the communications process goes wrong, then this can have very adverse effects on an organization.

Real advice, for the real world

The aim of this book is to look at the various elements of the communications process in the workplace, with particular emphasis on internal communications: if you cannot communicate successfully with people in your own organization then there is less chance you will be able to do so externally. The book will look at the various methods of communication that are available and also how to implement a communications strategy and evaluate the effectiveness of your communications process.

As with most things in the business world, there is a lot of theory about corporate communications, that does not necessarily translate to what is happening in the real world. But the art of good communications is to ensure that the right people get the right information, at the right time. It sounds simple and, if you do it right, it can be.

> The art of good communications is to ensure that the right people get the right information, at the right time

Knowing why you are communicating

Corporate communications is not something that should be done for the sake of it, or because your organization feels the need to have a communications section. You should have a clear idea about why you are communicating and this is why a communications strategy is important. This should tie-in with your organization's corporate objectives and set out a clear roadmap about how the communications process is going to help achieve these objectives.

Beware

One of the biggest mistake in communications is to think that it is something that will happen automatically. It takes a lot of planning, organization and evaluation to operate corporate communications successfully.

However, this is not to say that the communications process is all about high-level strategy, far from it. The way we all communicate in the workplace, from body language, to email, to written reports, has an impact on colleagues and, ultimately, the whole business.

Knowing how to communicate

In the modern world of communications, there are a vast array of tools at our disposal:

- Web
- Email
- Social media
- Video
- Paper
- One-to-one

All of these, and more, have an important part to play in corporate communications but they should not be viewed in isolation.

Being flexible

In the world of communications no two days are the same; you should always expect the unexpected. Because of this, you should always be ready to think on your feet and change your mind, and your plans, if necessary. This does not mean that you should change things at the drop of a hat, but you should always have the flexibility to assess a situation and move with events as they happen if required.

Honesty is the only policy

Being involved with communications in the workplace can be a powerful position as you have the chance to influence the way your organization operates. Therefore it is important that you are always open and honest in the way you communicate, either with individuals or with the organization as a whole.

Sometimes it may seem like the easy option to get out of a difficult situation, but if you are evasive or dishonest in the way in which you communicate you will undoubtedly get found out sooner or later. Once this trust is lost it is very hard to get back.

Ten Common Mistakes

It can sometimes be easy pointing out mistakes and none of us are perfect. The rest of the book aims to show how to avoid and overcome some of the issues that lead to ineffective communications in the workplace. However, the following are some of the areas in which people go wrong when they try and tackle the seemingly straightforward world of communications:

- Underestimating the complexity of the subject. Effective communications is a multi-faceted and multi-discipline function and anyone who thinks it can be mastered quickly and easily may be sadly disappointed

- Hiding behind corporate jargon. Corporate jargon is the scourge of the effective communicator. Always remember your audience and communicate at an appropriate level. The overuse of corporate jargon is frequently a sign of insecurity and this is used as a barrier to hide behind

- Letting work pile up. If you are disorganized then you will quickly become overcome with your workload and the communications process will suffer. If you cannot do something yourself do not be afraid to delegate it, with clear and appropriate instructions. Keep on top of emails, even if it  is just to get back to people to say that you are dealing with their enquiry and give them a timescale for when you will get back to them again. Leaving people not knowing what is going on is one of the worst things in communications

- Being indecisive. If you keep changing your mind, or cannot make it up in the first place, then you will create an atmosphere of confusion and resentment. Once you have made a decision, stick to it even if it ultimately may appear to be incorrect

- Making excuses. Even with the best intentions, things sometimes go wrong. If they do, the best thing is usually to accept responsibility and apologize. Do not try and blame other people as this will just breed mistrust and discontent

- Avoiding passing on bad news. Sometimes in the business world it is inevitable that you will have to give out bad news, either individually or as an organization. This should be approached head-on, but in as positive a way as possible

- Being afraid to ask for advice. Asking for a advice is not a sign of weakness, it is a sign of wanting to check to make sure you are doing things correctly

- Pretending to be an expert in everything. Due to the number of channels in the world of communications, no-one knows everything about every aspect of this discipline. One way to increase your own expertise is to be open and admit if you do not know everything about a certain area, rather than trying to just bluff it. This will not only improve your own knowledge but also gain greater respect from other people

- Thinking that style can make up for a lack of substance. It is important to make communications look stylish and attractive. However, this should not be at the expense of the message itself

- Ignoring your key customers. When communications go wrong it is frequently because the communicators think they are creating something just for the benefit of their boss or the people above them in the management chain i.e. they are just trying to impress their managers. However, the most important people are those for whom a message is intended. This is usually the rest of the staff in the organization and these should be considered your key customers

Don't forget

Good communicators do not necessarily have to be liked within an organization, but they definitely have to be respected in order to do an effective job.

11

Less is More

Frequently, when someone is asked to create a piece of communication, the immediate reaction is to produce something as long and complicated as possible. This is often driven by the person who has asked for the piece of work in the first place: since communications is viewed as being a very visual discipline a lot of managers and senior staff equate quality with the size of a document. In some cases, more emphasis is given to the weight of a document than to the content, almost literally in some cases.

> A lot of managers and senior staff equate quality with the size of a document

This can be seen as a lack of security by managers, as if they are seeking protection behind a wall of words. However, this can be a problem for the person creating the piece of work, since the aim of successful communications is to get your message across, rather than needlessly bumping up the word count for the sake of filling pages. Indeed, unnecessarily long documents can be counter-productive in terms of their usefulness. Even the most dedicated managers may find it hard to drag themselves through long documents, that are peppered with corporate jargon for good measure.

If you want to create documents that are meaningful and will get read, and hopefully acted upon, then think shorter rather than longer. This is a good discipline in terms of the size of the final document but it is also a good way to plan your writing. Before you start, note down the key points that you need to get across and also the conclusion that you want to deliver. This will then give your document a precise structure. When you start writing, stick to this structure and if a point only needs one paragraph then give it that and do not feel the need to pad something out just to make it look more impressive.

> Do not feel the need to pad something out just to make it look more impressive

Considering your audience

When creating communication documents, or online content, it is not only a question of keeping your superiors happy. At the end of the day, it is your target audience who will be your harshest critics if you do not get it right. So ultimately you have to tailor your writing and content for the people who will be consuming it.

When writing for your target audience there are a number of benefits in keeping things as tight and concise as possible:

- It should be easier to understand. If you cut out all of the unnecessary items in a document or report then you should be left with content that is clearer, since there are fewer redundant items

- There is less chance of confusion and misunderstanding if you stick to the key messages and these points are easier to identify. This should help people understand the messages and then act upon them correctly

- If you follow the 'less is more' philosophy, the end user should be able to consume the content quickly and then get on with other things. In this way clear communications should be seen as something that aids productivity as well as creating a better informed workforce

- You will begin to get the reputation as a clear communicator. This is something that can be hard to achieve but if people think you are giving them the right information in a digestible form then they will begin to start trusting your communication skills

Building on success

If you have produced a short, clear piece of communications that has gone down well with your target audience you can build on this success with future items. If there are follow-ups to the original item, these should be produced in the same style and issued whenever there is information to communicate: it is better to regularly issue shorter pieces of communications rather than save them up and lump them together in one document or report. But never become complacent: always look at any type of communications and ask yourself whether there is anything there that is redundant or not pulling its weight.

Don't forget

When you get something wrong there are usually people who are quick to tell you so. However, when you do something well the same is not always true. So, if you do not get any feedback from an item of communications that you have produced, this is probably a good sign.

13

Content is Still King

With the vast array of technology and communications channels now available to us it is easy to fall into the trap of thinking that it is just a question of pushing out our communications to these channels and letting the technology do the rest. However, this is a common mistake made by communications professionals: regardless of the number of channels, content is still king. The old adage, 'rubbish in, rubbish out' is as true today as it always has been – at the end of the day people want to get the best information possible and will quickly spot if you are trying to give them an inferior product.

Before you consider which channels you want to use for your message, you have to make sure that the message itself is what you want to convey. This involves considering some of these areas:

- Who is the audience? Knowing with whom you are communicating is important in identifying the type of content to be used

- Identifying what you want to say

- Adapting the length to the message

- Saying it with clarity

- Considering the format

Good content means saying the right thing at the right time. This could be a single sentence or a 30 minute video. The key is to know what you want to say and then say it as effectively as possible, using the available channels.

People will quickly identify good content and it will have two important effects: they will understand what you are trying to say to them and they will want to come back and see what else you want to tell them. This means that you have a receptive audience the next time you want to communicate a key message. However, this does not mean that you should become complacent: goodwill from an audience can be hard won, but it can be lost in a instant with a piece of poor or shoddy communication.

When creating content, remember to make every word, phrase and sentence count – if it is not needed, then leave it out.

Hot tip

Ideally, there should be a Content Editor in each Communications section. This role is responsible for checking content across all communication channels to ensure consistency and accuracy.

Setting Clear Objectives

Before you start creating any piece of communications, it is vital to have a clear objective of two things:

- The message you want to get across

- What you want to achieve with the message

So, if you want to communicate information about a change in an organization you will first have to identify the message. For instance, it could be a change in your organization's Absence Procedure.

Initially, the message would be the following:

- Inform people of the changes. It is important that people know about planned changes, before they happen. This will enable them to prepare themselves and take any steps that are necessary for when the changes take place

- Inform people of their responsibilities and those of their managers. Everyone has to know what their role is to be during any period of change and the communications that is associated with it. This is equally applicable if you are taking a passive role (just consuming the communications and information) or an active role (implementing the communications and changes)

- Detail any actions that have to be undertaken. Most objectives require actions to be taken to achieve them. This can range from someone reading a piece of communications aimed at them, to a team putting together a policy or procedure. This is another area that should be clearly defined, so that everyone knows what they are doing, and why

- Flag up the next stage of the process. Leaving people in limbo as to what is happening next can be the death knell for any communications process. Make sure that you have a clear timetable of what is going to happen and a timescale

Don't forget

Try and make the timescale realistic, but if it changes, don't be afraid to tell people this.

So the structure of the communications, in terms of main headings, could be:

- So What is Happening?

- Why is it Happening?

- What Do I Need to Do?

- What Does My Manager Need to Do?

- Timetable of Key Dates

- What Happens Next?

Once you have identified the message you want to get across you should identify your objectives in terms of what you want to achieve with the communications exercise. This should be done for both individuals and the organization as a whole. The objectives should be two-fold:

- Ensure everyone understands the message. This involves evaluating the message in terms of seeking feedback and holding follow-up exercises such as focus groups

- Use the message to bring about successful change in the organization. This is the ultimate goal and again requires some targeted evaluation at the end of the exercise

Beware

Communications is only something that you can make up as you go along if there is an emergency or a crisis. For all other occasions there has to be clear planning and objective setting.

Measurements could be put in place to find out if staff and managers are implementing the new Absence Procedure effectively, which would be an indication that the communications has been successful. Ultimately the objective should be to see that the level of absence has fallen in the organization, which would be an indication that the communications has contributed to a successful change.

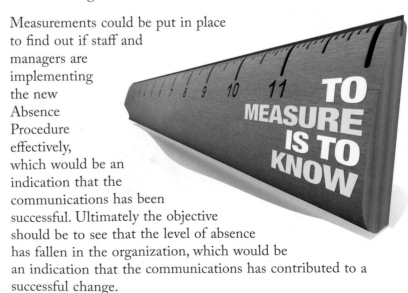

Getting the Right Team

Throughout our communication activities we must be ready and willing to react and innovate. In order to do so, we need to ensure that our communications team is connected to key areas throughout the business.

The team should be:

- Imaginative

- Creative

- Up to date with new technologies and therefore potential new channels

- Engaged and engaging

- Positive

- Respected by colleagues

- Open and approachable

- Flexible

However, especially in times when budgets are tight, we also require people who are:

- Pragmatic

- Have an understanding of the business context and corporate barriers and pressures

These characteristics and attributes are the key ingredients of communication teams which provide valuable business support.

As with all other areas of business; we are only as good as our people. Being involved at each stage, understanding our audience, evaluating our activities will all count for nothing if we have the wrong people involved.

Don't forget

A communications team should be just that: a team that works together and have the skills to stand in for each other, if required.

17

Creating Your Strategy

The first point to note when looking to create an effective communications strategy is that there is not a single approach which will work in all circumstances. Many organizations have a standard procedure which they use when communicating with colleagues and this procedure can be utilized without adequate thought given to the actual message being communicated.

Creating a communications strategy can be seen as a journey and, as with any journey, there are certain things that we need to understand and decide:

- Where we are currently

- Where we want to go

- How we intend to get there

It is inevitable that there will be obstacles along the way, however, by having the right tools and people at our disposal, an understanding of our environment and a clear map of our route; we can reach our goal.

Tailoring your approach

You may therefore hear talk of a single communications strategy and this "one size fits all" approach, while perhaps being suitable for everyday, straightforward pieces of communication, is not the way forward when dealing with communications in support of projects or business changes. You have to think of the best approach to fit the message, the aims and the audience.

> Think of approaching the development of a comms strategy as an art rather than a science

In fact, it is more appropriate to think of approaching the development of a comms strategy as an art rather than a science. The rigid step-by-step approach will not allow us to capture the essential requirements for each particular strategy. There needs to be creativity, imagination and flexibility when creating an effective communications strategy.

Don't forget

For more information about creating a communications strategy see Chapter Three.

An effective communications strategy will support the change being delivered throughout the lifecycle of that change: from the scoping/discovery phase, through development, implementation, evaluation and finally as we revisit the change in order to consider building and developing further.

Each stage will be supported by communication activities:

- Set the communication objectives, or goals – keep them SMART. This stands for: Specific, i.e. it has to be a clearly defined objective such as 'By the end of the year you will produce six training videos'; Measurable, i.e. it is something that you can measure or count once it has been completed; Achievable, i.e. it has to be something that you know the person is capable of doing; Realistic, i.e. you both have to agree that it can be done in the way it is set out; and Timely, i.e. there is a timeframe in which to achieve the objective

Hot tip

It is essential that objectives are measurable, so that you can display the value that they are delivering to the organization

- Ensure knowledge of subject, audience and context. It is essential that the communications team has a thorough understanding of these elements so that they can create the strategy accordingly and also respond to questions and feedback about different topics

- Sculpt the message. It is rare for a communications message to be perfect first time, so it is necessary to keep redrafting and evaluating until you are confident that you have the best final product possible

- Select the communication channels to be used. See Chapter Two for the range of channels that are potentially available

- Evaluate. This should be done throughout the process and you should not be afraid to change things as a result of feedback from evaluation

- Build and develop. This is the phase where you implement the elements of your communications strategy and start to create the different products

Measuring Success

It was Oscar Wilde who said, "What is a cynic? A man who knows the price of everything and the value of nothing." And that is the rub: how to do you measure and evaluate something as intangible as communications?

Proving value

Communication channels and activities are seen by some (we will call them cynics) to be expensive and unnecessary. It is not true of course, but at any time, and in particular in the current financial climate, it is vital to be able to prove the value of your Communications section and your comms channels. If you cannot, then be prepared to lose them.

> It is vital to be able to prove the value of your Communications section and your comms channels

For this reason it is crucial to introduce a degree of governance around all of your comms, whether it is for a single piece of communications, or communications for an entire project. Do not allow communications in support of a project to simply become a tick-the-box exercise. Project managers will be required to show that they have included their communications strategy in their project plan, but often this is done with no great conviction.

Get involved at project startup

Ensure from the outset that communications is represented on the project team and project board. Communications should not be an afterthought and something that is done just before a new project or initiative is launched. It should be embedded into the process from the start

and everyone should be aware of the importance of including communications.

Don't forget

For a detailed look at evaluation and measurement see Chapter Five.

20

Plan

It is absolutely imperative that all parties fully understand what is required from communications. Take time to plan your strategy:

- Agree on what the project expects from communications

- Who will be responsible for doing what

- What success will look like

- How this will be measured

Evaluate – Tweak – Evaluate

Projects come to an end and therefore communications relating to a project will be finite pieces of work. Our day to day channels, however, do not stop. A one-off evaluation of, for example, our intranet will lead to some conclusions and ideas for improvement. Once these improvements have been made do not think it is job done. Put in place a programme of evaluation and if something is not delivering do not be afraid to alter it, replace it or even remove it.

You cannot evaluate and improve everything continuously, but by following your program you can ensure a cycle of evaluation which tests each channel as regularly as required.

What makes something worthwhile?

Oscar Wilde would not have much time for modern day directors of finance. When it is all down to profit and loss it is very easy to see whether something delivers benefit. If the figure at the bottom is greater than the figure at the top then it is all rosy and we can normally carry on without that dreaded knock on our door.

...cont'd

Beyond the bottom line

The problem we have is that not everything boils down to the bottom line. Our project or comms channel may be designed to:

- Change staff/customer behavior

- Improve satisfaction in the workplace

- Improve the quality of work

- Or simply to inform

Success in these areas can be more difficult to demonstrate, but by defining and getting agreement on success up front we will have a strong foundation on which to build.

Hot tip

To find out more about Key Performance Indicators, speak to a project manager as they will work with these on a regular basis.

Another common problem can be a project which will run for a long period of time. We cannot afford to reach the end and realize that we have failed to achieve our stated communication objectives. In such a case it is advisable to set Key Performance Indicators (KPIs). These are our quantifiable critical success factors which are used to measure progress towards the stated final outcome. KPIs should be set within the project plan.

Why we evaluate

Evaluation provides the element of governance which helps us to know what works and what does not. It will provide the evidence we require to know whether an activity needs to be tweaked, removed or perhaps rolled out further.

More commonly these days, evaluation is the evidence we need to justify continued investment and is therefore a critical task in workplace communications.

Due to the nature of communications, evaluating it is not always an exact science and elements such as morale and organizational reputation should be considered. Therefore there should always be flexibility when considering the evaluation of communications.

Establishing Buy-in

If your audience does not believe what you are saying to them and, as a result, do not want to act upon it then this has serious consequences for the communications process and, ultimately, the whole organization. Staff have to have faith and belief in the communications process and it is essential to secure their buy-in to the way information is given to them. Establishing buy-in can be achieved by using some of the following:

- Showing the bigger picture. As communications objectives should be derived from the overall corporate objectives, it is important to communicate how certain things will help to achieve the bigger picture targets. For instance, if you are communicating about a new absence procedure, this should be shown to be an attempt to help individuals improve their own absences from work, which then help the business to be more productive and profitable, which ultimately is beneficial for all staff

- Answering, 'What's in it for me?' However altruistic we *help others* may claim to be at times, at the end of the day most of us want to know how certain objectives and initiatives are going to affect us individually. All communications should be aimed at showing how everyone will benefit from something, or at least how it will affect them. This may be in terms of explaining how organizational targets will benefit individuals, or showing how certain policies or initiatives will impact on the whole workforce

- Issuing regular updates. This is particularly important for initiatives that span a considerable period of time. If long periods elapse with no news being issued, then people will become frustrated about the lack of information and start to make up their own rumors and gossip. The best way to avoid this is to issue updates even when there has been no change. Be open and say this and, if necessary, explain why there has been no change. Set out a regular timetable for updates, and stick to it

Don't forget

When creating a piece of communication, think of directing it at an individual, rather than just the whole organization. This will help to give it a more personal feel.

Being Inclusive

Everyone in an organization is responsible for the communications process, whether they realize it or not. Whether it is consuming communications that is aimed at them, or communicating with their colleagues, every individual is involved in the way information travels around a business. Therefore, when you are involved directly in the communications process it is important to make everyone included in the process.

Creating a sense of ownership

Being inclusive means thinking of every individual in an organization and making sure that they are included in the communications process. This should then give them a sense of ownership and make them believe that what is being said is ultimately for their benefit. If you cannot take people along with you in the communications process, then it is doomed from the start.

If you cannot take people along with you in the communications process, then it is doomed from the start

Some ways in which people can feel they are being included in how things are communicated include:

- Taking people's views into account. Ask for feedback as frequently as possible, both in terms of the message that is being conveyed and also the method by which this is done. This will enable you to amend both, if required, based on what the staff say to you

- Acting on feedback. It is pointless, and indeed counter-productive, to ask for feedback and then not act on it. If there are certain things that you cannot do, then do not ask for feedback that could result in that reply

- Showing you have acted on feedback. Once you have received feedback and implemented any suggestions, it is important to highlight this: don't be shy about showing what you have done. This shows staff that they are being listened to and that their views are being taken into account and acted upon

Beware

One of the worst statements to hear in an organization is, 'There is no point making any suggestions because we won't be listened to anyway'. If you can actively show that this is not the case then you will have broken down an important barrier.

24

2 How we Communicate

Modern communications includes a wide range of potential channels: from the humble piece of paper to the exciting new world of social media. This chapter looks at the different options that are available and shows how they can be used together to deliver engaging communications.

Face to Face

Before technology came along to offer us almost limitless methods of communication, the one method that we had was communicating with each other face to face. Although this has been around since mankind first vocalized sounds, it is still one of the most effective means of communication and one that should definitely not been overlooked, even with the arrival of all of the new-fangled modern technology.

It's not all about the words

One of the reasons that face to face communication is so effective is that there are numerous factors that can help us interpret the message, in addition to what a person is saying. In fact, only a small percentage of a face to face message is conveyed by the words. The rest is done by:

- Facial expression

- Tone of voice

- Gestures

- Body language

When dealing with face to face communication it is a lot easier to interpret a message correctly as opposed to when it is written down, or emailed. For instance, if someone is talking to you and says, 'We need to have a meeting with the boss urgently' this could have different meanings depending on their tone and facial expression. If they are looking excited, happy and animated then it suggests that it is good news that they want to discuss.

Don't forget

When someone is talking to you, look at them to see how much you can interpret from non-verbal signals. The more you do this, the more subtleties and nuances you will begin to see.

26

gloom

If they are angry, downcast or <u>despondent</u> then it indicates the opposite. However, if this message was just written down then there would be no way of telling whether it was intended to be a good or a bad thing.

Note down the discussion

Despite the relative ease with which you can communicate face to face it does have a drawback: if there are debatable or <u>contentious</u> issues in the discussion these can cause disagreements at a later date, if the two parties involved disagree about what was said. It is therefore essential that you take a note of anything that was said in a discussion that could have ramifications for you and your work. If possible, send a note of the discussion to the other person and ask them to verify your recollection of the conversation. This can save significant problems and disagreements in the future:

leading to argument.

Hot tip

Email is a good way to get clarification of conversations and a physical record of them. However, do not feel that you have to do this for every conversation that you have.

27

Body Language

The study of our body language is a science in itself. Once you start learning about the signals that we give off by our expressions, gestures and movements you will never look at people in the same way again.

In terms of communication, our body language should be used to help get across the message that we are trying to convey. This can be done in a number of ways but the basic principle is to appear confident but not intimidating, so that other people can relax, listen to what you are saying and then feel comfortable about engaging in conversation.

Being open

One of the best ways to convey positive body language is to adopt an open posture when communicating with other people. This is opposed to a closed posture, which can appear intimidating and suggests disinterest. A closed posture includes:

- Crossing your arms

- Crossing your legs so that your body points away from people

- Arms and hands turned in towards your body

By contrast an open posture can put other people at ease and make communicating with them a lot easier.

Examples of an open posture include:

- Open arms with palms turned upwards

- Facing directly towards people

Matching people's actions

Despite our best intentions there will always be occasions when a certain degree of conflict is displayed in face to face communication. When this happens you should try and diffuse the situation rather than exacerbate it. However, this does not necessarily require a passive approach: the best way to do this is to match the other person's body language and tone of voice, and then slowly adopt a less aggressive attitude. Ideally, the other person will then copy your actions and temper their own body language. Of course, you have to be careful only to match the other person's body language and do not become more animated than they are or else you could make the situation worse.

Active listening

Body language can also play an important role when we are listening to other people. Generally, we look away from people when we talk to them and look at people when we are listening. When this happens, we should ensure that our body language indicates that we are listening to the other person and taking an interest in what they are saying. Some ways to do this include:

● Smile and nod your head at intervals to show you are listening and indicate agreement

Beware

Be careful not to crowd people's personal space by getting too close to them. This can make people feel nervous and defensive, which is not good for communications.

29

● Use facial expressions. It can be disheartening if you are talking to someone and they make no expression

Web

The Web has undoubtedly been the biggest development in corporate communications within the past 30 years. Millions of businesses, from the largest multi-nationals to sole traders, now have their own websites, to pass information to customers and also conduct business via eCommerce sites. In addition, a lot of organizations also have their own internal websites, intranets.

Evolution

The Web has come a long way from its infancy, when it was a novelty to see text from a website on screen, and a revelation to see an image slowly appear before our eyes. Now websites are multimedia rich in terms of images, animations and video.

However, with this evolution has come new challenges and some of the fundamental rules of designing websites are as relevant today as they always have been:

- Design sites for the benefit of the users, not for the ego of the Web designer

- Only include components if they are going to serve a specific purpose on your site. Do not add items just for the sake of it or because it is the latest development of Web design

- Simplicity is the key. It may be tempting to include every whizz-bang effect on your website just to grab people's attention. However, users tire of this type of thing very quickly and if they return to your site they will just want to be able to find the information they are looking for and as quickly as possible. The world's most popular website has fewer than 35 words on its homepage and one image.

Beware

The usefulness of a website is proved over a period of time, not just within the first few days when it is launched.

- Design websites that people will want to return to. The best way to ensure this is to update them on a regular basis. If users see a site is being maintained regularly then they will be more likely to return regularly too

- Navigation is a key part of any website. Invest as much time as you can to ensure that you have the best navigation you can on your website. This should include doing some research with the users to ascertain how they look for information and what they expect to find. (Remember, everyone looks for things in different ways)

Don't forget

For more information about website design, see Chapter Seven.

31

- Do not scrimp on the search engine. The art of searching on the Web has developed to a very sophisticated level and users now have much higher expectations in terms of using search engines to find content. Good search engines can be expensive but some investment should be made in this area to ensure the best user experience possible

Email

Email is one of the most ubiquitous communication tools in our working lives. Most office workers cannot go a day without checking and sending email, sometimes to people in the same room as them, or even at the next desk. However, although email can be a valuable device in the workplace there are also some risks attached to it and there are a number of considerations when trying to get the best out of it.

COMMON (handwritten annotation above "ubiquitous")

When the Internet was in its infancy, email was the function that became known as the first 'killer app' i.e. something that was so useful that it was going to attract a critical mass to this new communications tool so that it became widely accepted and used. Since then it has become part of our daily lives, whether we like it or not, particularly in the workplace.

Email and the Internet

People frequently refer to the Internet as the pages on the Web we all read everyday. However, technically the Internet is the worldwide system of connected computer networks that support Web pages and email, as well as other networked technologies.

Privacy

Emails are never private, even if you mark them as so, so do not put anything in an email that you would not want people other than the recipient to see. Think of the Sunday Newspaper Rule: don't put anything in an email that you would not mind seeing appear in a story in a Sunday newspaper.

It can be tempting to include light-hearted comments, or jokes, in emails, particularly with people you know well. However, if viewed out of context these types of comments can appear incriminating and even abusive at times. If relationships in the workplace break down then comments in emails can be used in any disciplinary actions that may be taken.

To be on the safe side, it is best to keep emails as functional as possible and keep the content to work matters.

Beware

Comments made in emails are frequently used in industrial tribunals. In this environment it is easy for the original meaning to be misinterpreted if it is taken out of context.

Benefits and issues

The benefits of email are obvious:

- It is instant

- You can contact a group of people at the same time

- You can include documents

- You have a record of discussions and decisions

However, it is also very easy to misuse email and the very things that make it so appealing can also create problems:

- Because it is so easy to use people come to over-rely on it and use it when other forms of communication are more appropriate

- Lack of context. Because email has no face to face element the meaning of the message can be misinterpreted. Words and phrases can be taken in the wrong way, leading to potential 'flame mail'. This is when electronic arguments start via email, frequently as a result of one person misunderstanding the meaning of something in a message

Words and phrases can be taken in the wrong way, leading to potential 'flame mail'

Hot tip

If you feel an email conversation is getting out of control, go and speak to the person, or people, in person. This can be the best way to clear up any uncertainty or misunderstandings.

33

- System overload. If a group of people are copied into an email, the temptation when replying is to include all of them using the Reply All function. Sometimes this is appropriate but at others it just creates ever-increasing numbers of emails as everyone else adopts the Reply All option. This also runs the risk of people seeing things that they should not

- Server overload. Emails take up space on your organization's servers in terms of sending and storing them. If large documents are attached this can slow down the system and will not endear you to your IT colleagues. A better option for this can be to store large documents in a shared folder, to which all of the relevant people have access

...cont'd

Etiquette and security

In addition to these issues, there are also others concerned with etiquette and security. These can have a major impact, for both the individual and the organization and, because of this, it is important to have the following in place:

- An email policy. This should cover the organization's approach to proper use of email and sanctions that are available if it is misused. It can be a standalone document and also incorporated into the company's Internet policy

- Email guide. This should be a guide on how to use email most effectively and get the most out of it as a business tool.

An email guide should include the following:

- Salutation. This should cover how you address people at the start of an email. Generally, the safest way to introduce an email is just to use the person's first name. If you are emailing a group of people you could use 'All' or 'Dear All'

- Length of emails. Since most people get a lot of emails during the working day it is best not to make them too long. Say what you need to say as concisely as possible: if you need to have a longer discussion, arrange a meeting with the person, or people, involved

- Formatting. This should include details of preferred font type and size and also the use of headings, sub-headings and bulletted or numbered lists

- Out of office details. This is the message that should be activated when a person is not available. It should be along the lines of, 'I am currently out of the office until [date]. I will be checking my emails occasionally but if your enquiry is urgent, please contact John Smith on 07878123456. Otherwise I will deal with your enquiry on my return'

- Email signatures. This is an automatic signature that can be added at the end of an email. Usually, it should include at least the person's name and job title

- Attachments. There should be clear guidelines about the size of attachments that can be sent. Check with your IT administrators to get this figure

Paper

One of the great myths of the computer age is the concept of the 'paper-less' office. When computers first came into our working lives it was claimed in some circles that this would lead to the extinction of paper in businesses and offices around the world. However, the opposite almost seems to be true and we are now surrounded by more paper than ever. The explanation for this is fairly simple: we like paper, it is simple to use, it doesn't crash or break down and we feel comfortable with it. We also equate it with work being done: when we see someone with a clipboard and a piece of paper we automatically think that they are engaged in some important business, even if in reality they are just writing their shopping list.

> We like paper, it is simple to use and we feel comfortable with it

Use it wisely

Despite the rise of technology there is still a important role for paper in the world of corporate communications. In meetings it is a lot easier to read a hard copy document rather than all crowding around a single laptop. Also, reading long documents is usually less of a strain if they are in paper format. However, this does not mean that paper should be used in an unthinking, wasteful manner. Some of the issues to consider are:

- Always ask yourself if paper is the most appropriate medium for a piece of work: could it be done better electronically or even face to face?

- Print documents double-sided, if possible, to save paper (also known as duplex printing)

- Keep scrap paper for note-taking

- Never equate the quality of a document to the amount of paper in it

Paper still has a valuable role to play in communications within the workplace, but we need to think carefully about how we use it and not automatically accept it as the default position.

Don't forget

Don't print out every email you receive and keep it in a folder, 'just in case'. Your IT system should backup and archive emails so you should be able to retrieve any if required

Social Media

Social media is the new kid on the communications block. As with a lot of innovative forms of communication, it started off as something of a novelty and then exploded onto the Web so that it was impossible to ignore. In a relatively short period of time it has evolved from being a tool for social interaction to a genuine communications tool for business.

What is social media?

The basic concept of social media is to provide a platform for people to share information and news with their friends and contacts. The most obvious example is now Facebook, which has evolved as the main player on the social media scene. Other sites such as YouTube for video and Twitter for text messages also inhabit the social media environment and provide yet more possibilities for getting your messages across to the world.

The biggest challenge for the corporate communicator is deciding how best to use social media in the workplace. Since it is such a new medium it can cause unease in a corporate environment and there are a number of issues that need to be considered:

● Do you really need to use social media? When a new innovation burst onto the scene the temptation is to use it just because it is there, particularly if you think everyone else is starting to use it. Because of the amount of publicity that social media has received it is easy to think that you have to get on the bandwagon or risk being left behind. Indeed, in the early days of social media a lot of businesses started using it precisely because it was there, without any long-term approach as to what they were going to do with it. However, as the technology has evolved and the users have become more used to social media tools it has now reached a level of sophistication where it is becoming a mainstream business communications tool. So it is not so much a question of whether you need it, but how you can use it for maximum impact

Hot tip

If you use social media sites as part of your overall communications, links to them can be placed on your website.

- Treat it in the same way as your other communication channels. If you are using social media you should not consider it a gimmick or an afterthought. It should be integrated into your overall communications strategy and used in conjunction with all of your other communication channels

- Create a social media strategy. It is not enough to use social media just because it is there and to tell people that your company has a Facebook page. You need to have a reason why you are using social media and this should be defined with a social media strategy. This should explain what you will be using social media for, which elements of social media you will be using and how it will tie-in with your other communication channels

Don't forget

Social media is definitely a generational form of communications. The younger generations feel more comfortable using it and this should be taken into account when you are developing a social media strategy.

37

- Create social media guidelines. Social media is fraught with danger in terms of people saying the wrong thing publicly. Barely a day goes by without a celebrity or someone in the public eye being in the news for something they have said on Facebook or Twitter. For personal use this is up to the individual, but for a business it can be extremely damaging if social media is misused. For this reason it is essential that you create guidelines that set out clearly how social media sites should be used within your organization. This should include details of who is allowed to publish information on social media sites, what type of information is and isn't allowed and sanctions that will be taken if people misuse the corporate social media sites

Posters

Posters may seem a slightly old fashioned form of communication when compared to the Web and social media sites, but they can be an extremely effective, and cost-effective, way of getting across key messages.

Poster sites

When using posters the first consideration should be where to locate them throughout the organization. The correct poster sites can make the difference between a message be conveyed throughout the organization, or being lost completely. When thinking about poster sites, take the following into consideration:

- Is it somewhere where the majority of staff will see it everyday? If not, it could be a waste of time, or even counter-productive if some people get the message and others do not

- Will people walk past it or do they have to stop there for some reason? Areas where people have to wait for a short period of time are ideal for posters; they can take in the message without having to interrupt something else

Beware

If you are displaying posters in public areas within your workplace, make sure that the content is suitable for the general public to see.

38

● Is it appropriate for a workplace message? Every worker likes to have a bit of down time during the day and so you should be careful not to encroach on this with workplace messages. For this reason, workplace restaurants or eating areas can be questionable for posters - it is a good chance to get the message across but will the audience be so receptive?

Some possible areas for poster sites are:

● Next to lifts. This can be a useful location as it gives people something to look at while they are waiting for a short time at a lift. However, this should still be long enough for them to consume the poster message

● Beside water coolers. This is a popular place for people to congregate in an office. Even though they may be deep in conversation about the sports results or the previous night's television, they may still take in any information on a nearby poster

Don't forget

Give someone the responsibility for managing and updating the poster sites around your organization. This should include a schedule of when different types of posters will be distributed.

39

● On noticeboards in open plan offices. These are generally located at the entrance to an open plan office and so people will see any posters when they enter or leave the room

● In the main reception area. If you work in a public office, reception areas can be used for posters for customers and the general public

Poster content

Content for posters can generally be broken down into two categories:

● One-off messages, such as a reminder for a specific event

● Messages that are part of an integrated campaign or strategy. This would be a series of posters that either convey the same message in different ways or separate elements of it

TV/Video

Using TV and video for corporate communications is an option that has significant pluses and minuses: on the plus side it can, if done properly, be an extremely powerful way to get messages across; but on the debit side, it is an expensive type of communication to both produce and distribute.

Creating video

Creating corporate video can be done on a small, consumer handycam video camera. This can work well for certain types of video, particularly those that are going to be distributed over the Web. However, if you are looking to produce a large volume of video then you may need to look at a more professional setup. This can be done by using professional video companies, but the cost for this will quickly mount up. Alternatively, you can set up your own functioning video studio. For this you will need:

- A suitable room. In most businesses there is considerable competition for room space and if you are pitching to use one as a video studio it will have to be a reasonable size. It will have to be able to accommodate all of the necessary equipment and also provide space for filming. It may also require seating for anyone who is going to be filmed, such as chairs and even couches

- Cameras. While you will not need top-of-the-range professional cameras, a step up from a handycam is best. A semi-professional level camera will do a very good job and you also  have to make sure it is not too complicated to operate so that a number of people can use it, if required. In addition to a camera, you will also need microphones and tripods

Hot tip

When buying cameras, also look at investing in an autocue system. This can be invaluable when filming scripted piece to camera, i.e. the participant is looking directly at the camera, rather than being interviewed.

- Lighting. If there is one thing that marks out a video as amateurish, it is the lack of proper lighting. If you want to create professional looking videos you will need to invest in some proper studio lighting. This can either be in the form of tripod-mounted lights or ones which are attached to the ceiling and controlled by a master mixing desk. Ideally, you will need a combination of both types of lights

- Sound-proofing. If you are lucky enough to be provided with a room for video work it is highly unlikely that it will be sound-proofed. This is another important feature as modern offices can be noisy places and you do not want unwanted background noise on your video. Sound-proofing is most effective over windows and doors, although ideally it should be around the whole room

- Background curtains. These can be used for backgrounds when shooting interviews and also for blacking out light from windows. Green background curtains can also be used  to achieve the 'green screen' effect. This is where the green background enables it to be removed in post-production and any other background dropped in instead

- Post-production equipment. This is used to create the final video once the footage has been captured. This should consist of a minimum of a high-spec computer, a video editing program such as Final Cut Pro, a large hard disk for storing the footage and final videos and a mixing desk. There are video companies that specialize in providing this type of equipment, but before you buy anything you should speak to them about your specific requirements

Beware

When using a green screen, make sure that the people being filmed do not wear anything green themselves. If they do, this part of them will disappear in the completed video as it will be removed along with the area of the green screen once edited.

...cont'd

Uses for video

The two main uses for video in the workplace are:

- Broadcasting news. This can be corporate news in the form of a news program with a presenter, or a message from a Chief Executive, or one-off programs about specific items. The advantage of this is that it shows real people throughout the organization and it is generally possible to give everyone the same message at the same time. Also, there is no chance of the message being misrepresented, which can sometimes be the case if something is passed on by word-of-mouth by a number of different people

- Providing training material. Video is an ideal way to distribute training material: it allows people to learn at their own speed, particularly as they can stop  the training video and then return to it when they want. Training videos on a variety of subjects can be purchased from training companies but it is also realistic to create your own. The advantage of this is that it will be tailored exactly to your business and the needs of your staff

Distributing video

Once video content has been created it can then be distributed throughout the organization. The two best ways of doing this are:

- Through desktop computers. This can be done with a video server and a media player on the computers. The issue of bandwidth is one that is important to consider, so that you do not overload your computer network

- Through a screen network of television screens. These can either be positioned statically at strategic locations or the screens can be put on stands and taken to the relevant areas as required

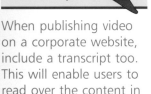

Hot tip

When publishing video on a corporate website, include a transcript too. This will enable users to read over the content in their own time. This can also make it available for blind or partially sighted users using a screen reader to read the text from the transcript.

Don't forget

For more information about creating and distributing video, see Chapter Ten.

Mobile Devices

With the proliferation of smartphones and now tablet computers, such as the iPad, the world of mobile communications in the workplace has well and truly arrived.

When dealing with mobile devices there are two areas to consider in terms of corporate communications:

- Websites
- Social media

Websites

Websites for mobile devices have to be designed specifically for this purpose, it is not just a case of designing a standard website and then have it displayed on a mobile device. This will lead to problems in the way it appears on the mobile device and in some cases it may not appear at all.

Websites for mobile devices have to optimized for use in this way and this is usually done by applying a specific stylesheet that is different from the one used for the standard website being viewed on a computer.

Social media

Mobile devices and social media are perfect bedfellows and a natural fit for corporate communications. As more and more people have smartphones and tablet computers it is now possible to target communications to these devices through sites such as Facebook and Twitter.

Users can consume their communications in this way and it is also an excellent way for producing communications on the move. It is no longer necessary to be sat at a computer in the office: you can use your mobile device to update social media sites, knowing that the information will be immediately available to the users.

In any communications strategy, mobile devices should now be considered with as much importance as any other channel.

Don't forget

A stylesheet is a set of formatting rules that can be applied to a single Web page or an entire website. Different stylesheets can be created for different types of devices.

Surveys

Feedback is an essential part of the communications process: if you do not ask people what they think, you will not know how to deliver what they want. One of the most effective ways of doing this is through surveys. This can be either online or as hard copy. However, the advantage of online surveys is that it is easier to analyze the results.

> If you do not ask people what they think, you will not know how to deliver what they want

Types of questions

There are a range of types of questions that can be used in surveys. These include:

- Multiple choice. These are questions where an answer has to be selected from two or more options. This can be a simple Yes or No question or have several options. Multiple choice questions can also be set up so that more than one response can be selected

- Rating scale, or grid, or matrix. These are questions where the reply is selected from a scale of options. This is used to assess the level of agreement for a statement. For instance, to the question, 'Should we all get paid more' the scale options could be Strongly Agree, Agree, Neither Agree nor Disagree, Disagree, Strongly Disagree. This then gives a range of opinions for a specific topic

- Open, or text. These are questions that require a textual answer. In general, these should be kept to a minimum and only used when there is a specific reason to do so

- Other. This is usually used to obtain additional information from a multiple choice answer. For instance, you may wish to find out why people answered No to a specific question. In which case an 'other' question could be used in the form of, 'If you answered No above, please explain your reasons'

When asking questions for surveys make sure that they are required i.e. you genuinely want to find out a specific question and you will be able to act on the answers.

Online surveys

Online surveys are a cost effective and efficient way to gather feedback from both internal and external customers. They can be hosted either on an external website or an intranet (depending on the type of software used to design the survey) with the replies coming back to a central point within the organization. The information can then be collated and analyzed using the software with which the survey was created.

Two options for creating online surveys are:

- Survey Monkey at www.surveymonkey.com. This is a complete online solution i.e. the survey is created and published online without the need to download additional software. Once a survey is completed a Web link is generated for the hosting of the survey. This link can then be sent to the people who will complete the survey

- Snap Surveys at www.snapsurveys.com. This is a separate program that is installed on your organization's system and then the surveys are created and published with this software

Online survey software has either customized templates to form the basis of a survey, or you can create your own from scratch. To do this, you can select the question that you want to ask and then select the question type e.g. multiple choice. You can then select the Answer options and apply other settings such as whether a question is mandatory i.e. it must have an answer.

> **Don't forget**
>
> Online survey templates can be customized to create your own look and feel and also include graphical elements such as your company logo.

45

Using Multiple Channels

With so many communication devices and channels it is easy to feel slightly overwhelmed by the available choices in terms of conveying messages and information. However, there are two important points to remember about this:

● Everyone consumes their communications in different ways

● There is no 'one size fits all' in terms of delivering communications. For each message, as many channels should be used as required and they should all complement each other in the delivery of the message

Integrating channels

When looking to communicate an item, whether it is a single, one-off item, or information about a major change or project, you should initially look at the message you want to get across and then design your communication channels around this. You can then select which parts of the message you want to be allocated to each channel. This could look something like this:

> You should initially look at the message you want to get across

● The headline message, and any background documentation, on the intranet

● Video interviews covering different aspects of the message. For instance, if it involves sections throughout the organization, have interviews with people from these sections, detail how the change will affect them and the impact it will have on the rest of the organization

● Headline messages on posters throughout the organization

● Face to face meetings if there are contentious issues that require questions and feedback

There should also be a timetable for when each message is going to be used on each channel. The main message should be published first and then supporting messages published at specific times to reinforce this.

3 Getting Strategic

Having a comprehensive communications strategy is essential for any organization. This chapter looks at the steps needed to create this and ensure it is fit for purpose.

Looking at the Big Picture

What makes a strategy?

The best analogy when we come to consider our communications strategy is to assess the journey we wish to make:

- Where are we now?

- Where do we want to be?

- How are we going to get there?

Not every change to be implemented in the workplace will require a strategy. However, every change will require to adhere to a strategy. So day to day communications to staff will be grouped together under an over-arching strategy. In the same way that we don't sit down each evening to create a route plan for getting ourselves to work the following morning we have, at some point, planned this journey and thereafter have applied that route on our daily travel.

> Every change will require to adhere to a strategy

Good and bad news

More important changes will require a bespoke strategy which will usually form part of an overall project plan. A major challenge for communicators in the current climate is that, very often, the change to be implemented will be considered unpopular.

Communicating good news should be relatively straightforward. However, when the message is an unpopular one the task for those in communications becomes more difficult, with knowledge of our audience and sensitivity around the message being conveyed taking on greater significance.

It is vital therefore that background work is carried out to help us prepare an effective strategy. This is the scoping phase where we define the following:

- The communications objective

- Identify and manage risks

- Set about ensuring that we understand our audience.

Don't forget

For more details about delivering bad news, see Chapter Four.

Setting Objectives

Scoping Phase

Many of you will no doubt be familiar with the idea of setting SMART objectives. This approach has become the norm in most areas of objective setting and it is no different in the communications sphere.

Let's remind ourselves what we mean by SMART objectives:

- Specific
- Measurable
- Achievable
- Realistic
- Timely

Defining objectives is the first and most crucial step in delivering a robust and effective communications strategy. These objectives, if defined correctly, will underpin the development of the strategy and plan. It is important, however, to remember that the objectives we set here are the communications objectives not the objectives of the policy or business change.

Introducing a change

Let us consider the introduction of a new IT Service Desk into our organization.

The business objective here is to implement a single contact point for all IT faults/queries.

Don't forget

Changes involving any other part of an organization will involve communications about what the change is and why it is taking place.

...cont'd

There will be a number of reasons why the business views this as a positive change and whilst we are not going to discuss these further, it is useful to note down several benefits which may have influenced this decision:

- Ensures that all faults are captured and logged

- Prevents staff from being taken away from issues on which they are currently working

- Delivers a fair method for the tackling of faults

- Helps to highlight equipment/systems which fail most often

- Allows tracking of call handling against Service Level Agreements

- Provides management information on number of calls/ time spent

It is immediately clear that none of the above would be considered communications objectives. Instead, these are the objectives of making the change. What might our communications objectives around this change look like?

- To ensure that staff are informed of new arrangements seven days prior to go-live.

- To ensure that members of staff in each business area receive contact details of the new Service Desk seven days prior to go-live and for one month following implementation

- Staff are informed two weeks prior to go-live how their calls will be handled by the Service Desk and what their role will be in ensuring its smooth operation

- Final reminder of new arrangements issued to all staff two days prior to implementation.

Beware

Having poor service from an IT Helpdesk can be one of the most frustrating things for people in an organization that relies heavily on computers.

50

Communicating the change

These objectives relate directly to how the change will be communicated. They comply with our SMART guidelines.

Note that raising awareness is not an objective as it lacks the clarity we require to deliver. What do we want people to do as a result of their increased awareness? Increased awareness is perhaps a stage our audience will go through, but it is not the final objective.

Communications can support the delivery of the policy objective or the business change by informing, reinforcing, motivating, normalizing or instructing.

Time spent on setting your communications objectives is time well spent

Time spent on setting your communications objectives is time well spent. Set time aside, bring key people into a room, bring lots of pens, paper and whiteboards and capture all ideas put forward. This is where you will establish the foundations on which your strategy will be built.

You will learn what needs to be communicated and will start to establish what political and social factors may have a bearing on your approach. You will consider your audience, you will begin to see how certain channels may lend themselves to the particular challenge you have in front of you and you will identify the barriers which may need to be tackled in order to succeed.

Don't forget

The SMART technique is also used frequently in staff assessment annual performance reviews.

51

Understanding the Audience

Identification of our target audience is relatively straightforward when dealing with an internal change. In our example we are clear that all staff must be aware of new arrangements and we can therefore presume that all staff make use of the IT infrastructure to some extent and will therefore require to log calls with the Service Desk. This will not always be the case however, even when all staff are involved; a degree of audience segmentation, based on our awareness of the various audience groups may be required.

Understanding our audience is vital and can have a significant impact on how we approach our communication of the policy or change.

Understanding your target audience

This is where our approach to putting our communications department together will demonstrate its worth. Having the right people in the communications team will help immensely when it comes to understanding your audience. Never underestimate the value of having staff in the team who have worked in other areas of your organization and have perhaps come up through the ranks.

Knowledge of your organization

Yes, often it is essential to recruit professionals in various fields from outside. However, think long and hard about your approach to filling vacancies in the communications team. Bringing an individual on board who has 20+ years in your organization and training that person to produce and edit your in-house magazine will demand expense and effort. Compare this to the approach where you recruit externally a person who has experience in this field and now you want to arm them with the knowledge and awareness which comes from having worked somewhere for 20+ years. Which is easier?

Along with that awareness and knowledge of the organization there also comes an understanding of colleagues:

- What motivates them?

- What has happened in the past which may have a bearing on how they will react to current changes?

- How does this change fit with the culture which exists in the organization?

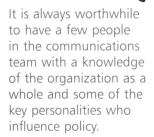

Hot tip

It is always worthwhile to have a few people in the communications team with a knowledge of the organization as a whole and some of the key personalities who influence policy.

Dealing with the unexpected

Like the comedian who cracks the wrong joke, to the wrong audience on the wrong night, it can be a long journey back from that tumbleweed moment when we get it wrong. It is probably fair to say that the biggest mistake you can make as a  communicator in any walk of life is to alienate your audience.

We are going to make mistakes, we know that before we set out and a technical fault which causes a video message to fail or a server crash which prevents a vital staff notice going out on time, sometimes just cannot be avoided. Hopefully, we learn something from it and we move on, a bit bruised perhaps, but a bit wiser also.

Displaying understanding

Leaving our audience with the feeling that we don't really understand them is probably the one mistake from which we will not recover. The alarming fact to note, however, is that this will have long-term ramifications for all of our future communications campaigns, it will not just impact on the strategy we are working on when the disaster strikes.

> Leaving our audience with the feeling that we don't really understand them is probably the one mistake from which we will not recover

Beware

Poor communications can have a serious impact on an organization in terms of staff morale and, ultimately, productivity.

Value your audience

So knowing your audience is essential to ensuring the successful implementation of elements of a communications strategy. They can get another internal communications team a lot more easily than you can get another audience.

Engaging the Audience

If the audience is not engaged with the communications process then it is doomed from the beginning. So we have to start by asking the following question:

● How engaged are the workforce with the policy/change?

Our level of understanding of our audience will play a large part in determining how accurately we will be able to predict their engagement with the policy or change that we are communicating.

Having the right people in our communications team will help with this. Our awareness of the organizational culture, our understanding of what this change will actually mean or how it will be perceived all provide us with valuable information and we must be actively using this information as we shape our approach and our message.

Doing the groundwork

Don't be lazy! Recycling a previous approach may work, but it should only be used if, having analyzed our task, we conclude that such an approach is the best fit. It should not be our default situation. Treat each policy/change as an individual piece of work using all relevant information to ensure that we have a tailored approach which takes into account how the message may be received and how engaged our audience members will be with what it actually means to them.

What are the barriers to participation?

"You never get a second chance to make a first impression." Will Rogers, the American actor/ comedian/cowboy/ politician (all round communicator) may or may not be the true owner of this famous saying (some dispute his ownership), but it is as true today as it was when it was first coined.

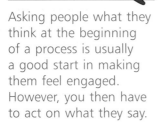

Hot tip

Asking people what they think at the beginning of a process is usually a good start in making them feel engaged. However, you then have to act on what they say.

54

Avoiding barriers

As communicators, we are the link between the audience and the message. One small error of judgement, one perceived lack of understanding, an ill-advised quip, a misjudged tone; anything which leaves our audience feeling that we do not actually understand them can see the communicator becoming a barrier to audience participation. As author Maya Angelou said, "People will forget what you said, people will forget what you did, but people will never forget how you made them feel."

> We are the link between the audience and the message

Our organizational culture can often be a barrier to staff supporting a new initiative. What are others saying? How will they be viewed by colleagues if they buy into something which the majority oppose?

The wider impact

What about the wider ramifications of the change? A change in practice may mean additional responsibility for one area, but a reduction in the role of another. This could make it difficult for staff in the area which is seen to be benefitting as they may feel that they are being disloyal to colleagues. Their feeling uncomfortable with the wider impact of the change may become a barrier to effective communication, as they disengage rather than support it.

Even when dealing with internal changes we may need to tailor our message to suit different sections within our organization. While we may be more accustomed to using audience segmentation when dealing with external communication campaigns, it can also be used very effectively internally.

Of course, we want to relay a consistent and honest message to all staff. However, dividing the audience groups, based on what the change will mean to them, allows us to address their specific concerns and home in on the details which are important to each group. The overall change is the same but, by using our understanding of the audience, we will have the ability to zone in on the information which they consider to be most important.

Don't forget

One of the most powerful methods of communication is word of mouth. If you are told something by a colleague you may react much more favorably than hearing it through official channels.

55

Influencing Behavior

The study of Behavioral Science, our understanding of it and how it can be applied has grown incredibly in recent years. However, advertisers have been using it for decades as they set about applying it in order to influence their potential customers' behavior.

There are many factors which may influence how we may react to a particular message.

Let us briefly consider the introduction of our new IT Service Desk. How might our understanding of Behavioral Science help shape our strategy?

Hot tip

If you are giving examples to illustrate a point, try and make them realistic ones so that people can identify with them.

1. We are heavily influenced by who communicates the information	
	Ensure staff notices relating to change are owned by Senior IT Director
2. We respond to incentives. E.g. we are more likely to keep a dental appointment if there is a charge for canceling	
	Short video placed on intranet to show how a call not logged in the new way will not be assigned a reference or a priority. Calls then not picked up by Service Desk staff and consequently will go unnoticed. Those logged afterwards, and perhaps relating to less important issues, will be tackled and closed while our issue remains.
3. We are strongly influenced by wishing to fit in with the majority	
	Posters to be displayed in work areas showing weekly stats on number of calls logged with Service Desk during previous week to show the level of participation.
4. We tend to go with the flow rather than being seen to opt out	
	Introduce a button on the intranet which links automatically to an email address for new Service Desk.

5. We are more likely to engage if the message is relevant to us	
	Use staff from various work areas in our posters. Use real life issues from various work areas in our video.
6. Our behavior can be influenced by prompts which suggest to us that it is okay to behave in a certain way. E.g. we see litter lying around and are therefore more likely to see it being "okay" to drop our litter	
	Have pre go-live meetings with managers from each area to ensure that they support the initiative and are seen to be contacting the Service Desk in keeping with the new directive.
7. Emotional associations can influence how we will behave	
	Show on video the impact of a call being missed. Perhaps the end customer does not get the service they required. Show the real life impact of this e.g. our member of staff could not open a particular customer record, logged call with Service Desk incorrectly. Customer therefore did not receive goods or help needed meaning disruption to their plans, child's birthday present not delivered, car not fixed meaning missed hospital visit.
8. Having contracted to a particular agreement or code of conduct we seek to honor this commitment	
	Reinforce message with individual email to all staff. Include a respond button which has to be clicked to show that email has been read and understood.
9. We tend to act in ways which make us feel better about ourselves	
	Show on video the impact of getting it right. Take examples from "Affects" and show how things went well when our colleague followed correct procedure.

Selecting Channels

Okay, so we know our audience, we are clear on the message. Now let's just get it out there so that people know what is going on.

But let's hold on a minute. This is where we require another piece of planning which will build on what we already know. Just as our tone and how we structure the content of the message are vital, so too is the delivery method we opt for.

What channels might be available?

- Electronic – e.g. intranet, staff forum, blogs, eZine, video, emails, screensavers, desktop backgrounds, voicemail

- Face to face – staff meetings, manager meetings in order to cascade information, conferences, seminars

- Print – staff magazine, posters, memos, one to one handouts

Don't forget

Different channels should not be viewed in isolation, but seen as connecting elements in an overall strategy.

- Environmental – white boards, noticeboards, mousemats

- Informal – chats between colleagues, coffee breaks, pre/post meeting discussions

Concentrating on the substance

The channel(s) we select will require differing approaches, however it is extremely important not to make the 'style over substance' mistake. Modern day communication channels provide us with tools and gadgets that can be extremely fun and interesting to use. However, we must ensure that we concentrate on our strategic aims rather than becoming too preoccupied with the potential of the technology or the style and design of the message. Style and design are important, but the message is key.

Style and design are important, but the message is key

The most appropriate channels will vary in line with many other factors including:

- Target audience

- Importance of message

- Sensitivity of message

- Budget

- Timescale

- Potential impact

- Mood in workplace

Don't forget

Start by getting the right message and then decide how best to communicate it.

...cont'd

● Political environment

● Perception of channel

The last one may seem odd, however you may find that people have very strong views on communication channels. Some people will view a staff forum as being inappropriate as it may include threads which seem frivolous or non-work related. Others will see video as being expensive, a gimmick and a distraction from the day to day business. It is important to be aware of your staff's perception of each channel and to use channels effectively and when appropriate. Failure to keep this in mind will, ironically, result in your communications channel becoming a barrier to getting your message across.

> It is important to be aware of your staff's perception of each channel

Corporate culture

The mood in the workplace can play a big part in the effectiveness of individual channels. Colleagues may react badly to being called to staff meetings if they are, at the same time, coming under pressure to increase output.

An email or staff notice which allows the individual to consume the information when it suits them may prove much more popular. Conversely, the directive stating that we need to up productivity may not be fully embraced if it is simply delivered via email or a staff notice without giving staff the opportunity to discuss it further at group meetings.

Beware

Always deal with the most important messages first: staff may not be too interested in the office chairs being replaced if they are worried about a major reorganization that is being considered.

Money, money, money

It is important to be mindful of budgetary constraints when selecting your channels and how this will affect your choices. It is obvious that we cannot create expensive videos and interactive Web-based communications if we lack the budget.

Consider also the overall fiscal position of your organization and the political landscape when selecting which channels are appropriate. You may have the money in your budget, but if other areas are being cut to the bone they may not be wholly receptive to your latest video production or eZine.

Don't forget

Try and save money wherever possible, but do not do it at the expense of compromising your key communication messages or methods.

61

Using channels wisely

So channel selection will often be as much about how well you know your audience, as it will be about how skilled you are with your channel. It will hinge greatly on the message being relayed, the sensitivity of this message and how staff may react. It comes back once again to ensuring that you have the right people. You need staff with strong networks within the workplace, staff who can provide a good barometer of opinion and on how a particular message will be received.

It comes back once again to ensuring that you have the right people

Changing Behavior

We spend a large proportion of our week at work and yet so many people refuse to engage and act in a way which makes that time enjoyable. In fact, many people find themselves in an environment which is extremely negative and energy sapping.

How our colleagues behave can have a huge bearing on how we view our work. The thought of getting up each morning to head into a workplace where the overwhelming mood is one of negativity is no fun and yet it is so very often the reality.

Increasing staff engagement

Communications has a pivotal role to play in increasing the engagement of staff. We can achieve great things when we have the right people involved and understand our audience. Often, as well as trying to bring staff on board with workplace initiatives, we can influence behavior in other areas.

Hot tip

Staff engagement is a major topic in the corporate world and some organizations have specific posts, or whole sections, dedicated to working on this.

62

Effective communications can change lives. You will have encountered some pretty major communication campaigns which have been designed to address key issues in society. You may not even have thought about them in this context previously, but they demonstrate the impact that well planned strategies can have.

Effective communications can change lives

Impact of campaigns

Think about a Government campaign to tackle domestic violence. Here we have such a serious issue which has to be handled in a particular way in order to yield positive results. The campaign's impact can be massive, however it also deals with a sensitive, potentially life or death, issue. So what would you do?

As stated throughout this chapter it is vitally important to know your audience; a campaign such as this demonstrates perfectly why this is the case. Knowing the subject matter has also been stressed as has having the right people involved. So clearly, the correct approach here would be to engage with experts in this area. This will help us to understand the subject and the audience. This understanding will then point us in the right direction when it comes to channel selection and the tone of our message.

It is easy to view these high profile campaigns as just being high visibility, wide-reaching public information initiatives. However, the work outlined above has been done in great detail in order to design a campaign which delivers.

Assessing background information

So what did the background work tell us?

The analysis showed that in the vast majority of cases of domestic violence the victims are women. This fact alone pointed the communications in a particular direction with poster sites chosen for their proximity to locations where women might be more likely to visit e.g. nurseries, health clinics. The background work also identified that information around such a topic is considered more effective when we engage one-to-one.

So, posters are effective, radio ads are effective as radio is often listened to when we are alone e.g. on in the background at home, in the car etc. The placing of posters in tube/subway trains or buses delivered positive results as, again, we are often alone when traveling on public transport and tend to look at and read posters in these types of locations as we strenuously endeavor to avoid making eye contact with our fellow passengers.

Aims of communication campaigns

What was the intention of the campaign? The ultimate aim of the Government was to reduce domestic violence. However, the aim of the communication campaign was to create an environment where our audience was aware of the full range of support mechanisms that were in place, that audience members were aware how to make contact with these and that they were confident that all contact would

They were confident that all contact would be kept confidential

be kept confidential. Evaluation of all channels was also planned up front so that the campaign could be tweaked as it progressed in order to yield maximum benefit.

You will probably not deal with such serious issues in your communications, but what can we learn from such weighty campaigns that might help us change behavior in the workplace?

Hot tip

Look at other campaigns, such as advertising campaigns on television, to see the techniques that they use to catch, and hold, our attention.

Running a Campaign

Consider how we might approach a campaign at work which is designed to promote a healthier lifestyle to our staff. Why might this be something our employer would wish to promote? How might they choose to endorse this?

A healthier workforce is a happier workforce. It sounds very clichéd, but it is undoubtedly true. As an individual, do you generally feel happier when you are healthy or when you are feeling under the weather?

Increasing productivity

A healthier workforce will almost certainly mean more productivity from those who attend work and will also, just as surely, mean that more of us actually do attend work.

Therefore, we can probably reasonably surmise that it benefits our organization if our colleagues are healthy.

So we have decided that we would like to help promote a healthy lifestyle among our staff. We can start this by identifying who will be the overall owner of this initiative.

Identifying owners

A likely owner of this campaign would be our HR department, if this is where our Health and Safety Team sits. So we decide to launch an initiative to promote a healthy approach to life and we decide that this campaign will be owned by our HR department. A small project team is formed, but this campaign is going to rely heavily on strong, well thought-out communications.

This campaign is going to rely heavily on strong, well thought-out communications

Our communications department is therefore included in the project team from day one. Our initial task is to understand what the campaign hopes to achieve and we can then set about planning how we will contribute to its success. We know the audience, we know the organizational culture and we know our available channels.

Don't forget

Any campaign that needs the involvement of communications should be part of the overall strategy of the organization.

64

Identifying campaign aims

The first task is to identify what we want to achieve from a campaign:

- Reduced sick absence

- Increased productivity

- Increased staff satisfaction (happiness)

How do we aim to achieve these?

- Promotion of a healthier diet

- More exercise

- Health and wellbeing support

- Health checkups

Audience

Next we need to specify the target audience:

- All staff members

At times there may be campaigns that are targeted at specific groups but, generally, they will be aimed at everyone.

...cont'd

Channels Available

Once we have identified the aims and the audience we can select the channels that are going to be used:

- Meetings
- Staff Notices
- Posters
- Video
- Social Media
- On-line staff magazine

We put together the following:

Don't forget

It is essential to have buy-in from senior managers for any campaign, otherwise the rest of the workforce will question why they should do it.

1. An initial staff notice informing staff of our organization's support of this initiative

2. A meeting/workshop to which we invite a number of health and fitness sector companies and we ensure senior managers participate in these

3. A series of posters which push behavioral changes:

    a. Why Not use the stairs?

    b. Why Not choose the healthy menu option?

    c. Take part in our free health check up

    d. Offer 25% reduction for local gym membership

    e. Pick up a free step counter for our walking challenge

4. A video featuring staff talking about the lifestyle changes they have made and the benefits they feel they have derived

5 Create a dedicated area on our staff forum for staff to discuss how they are participating

6 Regular slot in staff magazine dedicated to health and wellbeing where:

> a. Staff discuss their progress
>
> b. Local health clubs advertise what they can offer
>
> c. Healthy recipes are published

Putting it all together

You will see that we are communicating in ways which utilize many of our available channels and seek to achieve our aims:

- We have ensured various messages are delivered by experts on the subject

- We offer incentives designed to encourage staff to participate

- Providing channels for staff to discuss their progress help this new approach to be seen as the norm

- We have designed our own bespoke campaign so the message is relevant to our staff

- We ensure early buy-in from senior managers and early involvement of staff at workshops

- Lots of channels provided for staff to discuss how their engagement has helped produce positive results

- Ideas such as the gym membership and step counters encourage a feeling of having committed and contracted to actively take part

- The whole campaign is supported by channels allowing staff to discuss progress and feel good about taking part

Hot tip

Everyone likes to get something for free, so offering goody bags as part of a campaign is an excellent way to initially engage with people. However, this then has to be followed up by an effective campaign.

The Message is Key

Perhaps the most important thing to note is that the campaign has been designed for this particular initiative in a way which promotes the message we are relaying and supporting.

It is all too common for the strategy to be constructed in order to fit the channels, whereas our channels should be available to be used by each campaign and should be flexible enough to be driven by the strategy. It is tempting, having purchased capabilities around a new staff magazine or an on-line forum, to be absolutely determined to use these come what may.

This is usually in an attempt to justify the investment we have made in these tools, however, this approach will undoubtedly be counter-productive. Our audience will, in all likelihood, detect immediately that this is what we are doing. They will see it as a determination to use our new 'gadgets' and this will detract their focus from the message we are putting across.

The channels must accommodate the message, not the reverse.

In summary

So in order to start putting together your communications strategy you need to do the following:

- Know the message

- Identify the audience

- Understand the culture

- Utilize the channels available

- Understand where you are

- Identify where you are going

- Plan how you intend to get there

Once these things are in place your strategy can start to take shape. It is not necessarily a quick and easy process to put a strategy together. However, if you are committed to it and perform it in a thorough and professional manner then you will have the foundations on which all of your communications can be based. Having a robust strategy in place is the bedrock on which you can then produce diverse and engaging communications.

Beware

People are becoming increasingly sophisticated about communications these days so do not try and pull the wool over their eyes as they will see through it very quickly.

4 Communicating Change

Communicating change is one of the biggest challenges in the business world. This chapter shows how it can be done to achieve positive and lasting benefits.

Change is Constant

Some people don't like change; it scares them. Others embrace it and see it as an opportunity for development, advancement and even excitement. In the world of business, change is not only constant and inevitable, it is also necessary and desirable. History is littered with examples of businesses that did not change with the times, or changed too slowly, and were out-maneuvered by their competitors.

History is littered with examples of businesses that did not change with the times

Don't forget

Change should always be promoted as a positive thing in an organization. If you don't change, you stagnate instead.

Why change is good

Even though everyone may not be a fan of change, at least initially, there are a number of reasons why it should be seen as a good thing:

- It makes us think about what we do currently. No system or process is ever perfect, so when changes are introduced it gives us a chance to see how we can improve what we do

- It introduces new ideas. Everyone should always be open to new ideas and periods of change allow us to think differently and try out some new ideas and initiatives

- It challenges us to learn new skills. At times of change, those who usually survive the best, and flourish, are those who adapt, learn new skills and use these to make the most of any changes that are taking place

Introducing change

Even when we accept that change is a good thing, it does not mean that changes should be introduced without any communications and just hope that everyone likes them. There should be a clear strategy for communicating any major change in an organization. This should include the following:

- Why it is being done

- How it is being done, including a timetable of events

- The benefits that it is intended to achieve

Including Everyone

Change is not something that happens to other people in an organization, it happens to everyone. Even if it is a change affecting a specific individual, this can also have a knock-on affect on other people. But as far as corporate change is concerned, it is essential that everyone is considered and included in the process.

Planning for change

When a significant change is being planned, such as a major reorganization of the business, the first step is to plan how the change is going to take place. This will include the issues on the previous page for introducing change and it should also include a plan for letting the workforce know and showing how it will impact on them.

Letting everyone know

If people do not know about change before it happens then they are much less likely to embrace it enthusiastically. Therefore there should be a clear program of communications to let people know about the change. This could include some of the following:

- Intranet. Include full details of the change here, including background information, a timetable for what is going to happen and the intended outcomes

- Meetings. When dealing with change, people like to hear about things face to face and have the chance to ask questions and clarify points

- Posters. Use these around the organization for key messages and reminders about specific events and milestones

- Postcards. These can be distributed to staff with a timetable of events and dates for when changes are going to take place

- Video messages. These can be produced to reinforce the messages on the intranet. Separate videos can be produced for specific elements of the change

Hot tip

Try holding some focus groups before you implement any major change. This way you will get an idea of what people think about it and so be better prepared when you are communicating with the whole workforce.

Developing a Change Plan

When deciding on an approach to a Change Communications Plan you should start with one little word: Why? (Okay, one little word and a question mark.)

You need to be clear on why you are delivering a change in your approach to an aspect of our business. You need to articulate this to the business by using available channels effectively and appropriately, but being absolutely consistent and unambiguous on the reasons for the change is critical.

Four tasks

Being clear on what is going to happen, and why it is going to happen, allows you to tackle the first of four tasks which together will inform your Communications Plan:

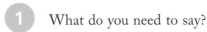

1 What do you need to say?

Your next task is to identify every group who has an interest in the change: the stakeholders. So this is our next question:

2 To whom are we saying it? Perhaps more correctly, with whom are we communicating?

The answer to our next question will alter for each stakeholder group and will also vary with the stage of the change and the information being communicated:

3 What channels will we use to communicate?

And finally, just as the pace of the change is important; so too the timing of our communications is absolutely key:

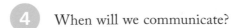

4 When will we communicate?

Don't forget

Speak to all of the relevant stakeholders face to face, rather than trying to find out their requirements by email or over the phone.

Taking your time

Time spent in answering the above questions at the outset is time well spent. All too often, Communication Plans follow a generic formula or are hastily put together so that the Project Manager can tick a box and assure his Project Board that the communications are in hand. Take time to do it properly. You will be sure to reap the rewards as the project progresses.

Goals

Having established what we are saying, and to whom, our next step is to break the overall communication needs into goals. These goals will be our targets at different stages of the project:

- Inform people of the change

- Check on their understanding of the reasons behind the change and what benefits it will deliver

- Seek their opinion. Do they agree with the change?

- Seek their input. Can they help implement the change?

- Inform them of our progress

- Check again on their understanding. Do they know what stage we have reached?

- Publish early results

- Check on awareness of these results

- What do they think of the change?

- Capture ideas for further improvement

Don't forget

It is essential that people fully understand why a change is being made from the outset. Otherwise they will go through the rest of the process as a token gesture for ticking boxes.

73

...cont'd

Channel selection

It is tempting to say that different stakeholder groups will respond better to different channels, however, this is too simplistic a view. Within each group, channels may be more popular with subsets of these groups e.g. if we have staff based in our head office who carry out a particular role, and staff based remotely who perform the same role, we may well find that head office staff will be happy with a staff notice as they regularly meet project staff and receive informal updates. Staff based remotely, however, may feel that update meetings with senior managers are required to ensure that they are being kept in the loop.

The explosion in social media also highlights how the age demographic within various stakeholder groups may guide our channel selection. We may find that we communicate via social media to 18–24 year olds in several groups, but that other age brackets within these stakeholder groups will prefer more traditional channels.

Don't forget

Make sure you use the appropriate channels for the message you want to convey. Do not use something just because it is there.

Fail to plan: plan to fail

Without a robust Communications Plan we will almost certainly compromise the success of the project as:

- Staff feel that their views are not valued

- We create a feeling of things being done to people rather than with them

- Changes cause confusion

- We lose out on valuable feedback

- We deny ourselves access to staff who may be able to help progress the change

Delivering Bad News

In the corporate world, as in life, it is inevitable that there will be times where we will have to deliver bad news. This could be on an individual basis e.g. someone has not got a promotion for which they have applied, or on a corporate basis e.g. the workforce is going to have to be trimmed as a result of falling orders.

How not to do it
No-one likes giving negative news and because of this it is frequently handled badly. Some examples of this are:

- The ostrich approach. Putting your head in the sand will not make the problem go away, it will just make it much harder when it is delivered

- The evasive approach. Delivering bad news in evasive terms just makes people feel more confused, unsure and stressed

- The dishonest approach. Unfortunately, some people will say almost anything to get out of an awkward situation. However, this will not change the reality of the situation and cause considerable disharmony and distrust

Being realistic
When you have to deliver bad news there are some steps that you can take to try and make the process as acceptable as possible:

- Preparation. When there is bad news to deliver there will inevitably be questions and concerns. Therefore it is essential that you prepare yourself with as much information as possible, in terms of background details and what will be happening next

- Clarity. Be as clear and straightforward as you can. There is no point in trying to make the bad news sound like something it is not and people will appreciate if you give the news as it is, without trying to dress it up in any way

- Honesty. As well as being clear, it is also essential to be honest. Give all of the facts that you have, even if some of them are upsetting or worrying

- Positivity. In most situation there are some positives that can be found. Do not make these up, but try and find some positives, such as re-training or different job opportunities

Beware

If you are delivering bad news to an individual be prepared for an adverse reaction. However well you deliver it, bad news is still bad news.

Evaluating Change

The evaluation of change is often described in a way which makes it seem much more complicated than it needs to be. We make changes every day, we evaluate the changes we have made and we decide if the changes were worthwhile. In doing so we do not feel the need to get overly theoretical. We talk in straightforward language and describe why we thought the changes were necessary and whether we realized our goals.

That is how it works in our day to day lives. Yet, for some reason we often lose sight of this in the workplace. Let us look at a real-life example of dealing with a change:

- I receive an invitation to attend a promotion interview and decide to buy a new suit as my current one has seen better days. So here is my change initiator and my benchmark

- I set my budget

- I decide on the style and quality I require

- What about a new shirt, tie, shoes?

- I shop around, decide on my best option and make my purchase of a new suit

- I attend my interview and guess what?

Don't forget

For more information about evaluation see Chapter Five.

Don't forget

We all undergo changes and evaluate them everyday. This does not have to be on a major strategic level, it could just be which sandwich to have for lunch. However, it is important to recognize the processes involved.

This is an everyday example of a change and mirrors exactly the circumstances surrounding a change in the workplace:

- We identify a need and set our goals

- We specify our requirements

- We capture any dependencies

- We implement the change

- We evaluate

The success, or otherwise, of my analogous new suit will probably hinge on the result of that interview. I could however have decided that, irrespective of my interview result, I will be happy with my purchase if I feel good about myself, people comment on my smart appearance, the old one had served its purpose and this one was needed, it fits well and looks great.

We can therefore evaluate changes in different ways:

- Improved profitability

- Reputational benefit

- Compliance to standards

- Increased staff or customer satisfaction

The key is:

- To know where you started

- Understand the need for change

- Agree up front on what success will look like

- Deliver the change and assess it against stated goals whether it is a suit, a new IT system or a process change

Beware

Without evaluation, important benefits resulting from a change could be missed.

Setting the Pace of Change

The role of communications in setting an appropriate pace for change is crucial. As the link between the business and the staff, your communications team has to have a sound understanding of your organizational culture. It is your "ear to the ground" and should be positioned to advise on the prevailing mood. We have talked extensively of the need to know your audience and your communications team has responsibility for this task.

The difficulty for many senior managers is to trust the barometer reading provided by the communications team. All too often, your communications team is seen as having responsibility for delivering the message but, remember, communications is two-way. Therefore it is imperative that you trust the messages you receive back to your communications team, otherwise why should your staff trust the messages going the other way?

Defining change

The communications team should be empowered when it comes to setting the pace of change and they should be trusted to deliver this. An organization which presses ahead with a change programme, without first having sought the views of staff and taken time to explain the route it is taking, will run a very high risk of losing the confidence of its people. However, it is perhaps more of a risk

> The communications team should be empowered when it comes to setting the pace of change

if we are seen as being heavy legged in our approach to change. Setting expectations, getting people on board and then adopting a slow and overly prescriptive approach can lead to the audience becoming sceptical and confused.

Understand the mood in the camp and be open and honest. As a member of the communications team; be an effective communicator with senior managers as well as colleagues in the business. The information you provide upwards will help set an appropriate pace of change which allows change to progress, but also ensures buy-in from staff. In a time of change, good communications keeps things moving along.

Embedding a Change Culture

There are a number of organizational behaviors which will ultimately make or break our attempts to embed a change culture.

Commitment

Are managers and team leaders at all levels on board?

Failure to secure buy-in from managers will almost certainly result in us not achieving our aims. All too often we see managers who appear to embrace the culture of change, but whose words and actions, when involving their own staff in the initiative, betray a negative attitude and a lack of engagement. We need everybody pulling in the same direction.

Share the vision

Set a realistic timetable with short term goals defined.

We discussed earlier how setting the appropriate pace of change is absolutely essential. Do not be pressured into setting targets which are almost impossible to achieve. Let the changes settle in at a pace which allows them to be adopted through a natural process, do not push for too much too soon. At the same time do not set target dates which stretch almost out of sight into the future. Aim for short term indicators which will highlight whether we are on the right track towards our more long-term goals.

Don't forget

Embedding a change culture is something that will only happen over a period of times, usually a number of years. Results will be seen slowly so do not expect too much too soon in this respect.

Keep it simple

The principles around why change is required tend to be straightforward.

Define communication and engagement strategies which deal with the fundamental questions. Why? Who? What? When? How? Develop plans which are appropriate to the change and take time at the outset to ensure these plans meet our needs.

Be inclusive

For staff and stakeholders to feel part of the process they must be participants. Not victims!

It may sound dramatic, but all too often stakeholders are made to feel that they have been steamrollered by changes which they did not see coming and in which they have not had an opportunity to participate. Do not just hold staff workshops and opinion surveys in order to say that you did so. Actively engage with stakeholders and value their input.

Channel selection

You have a wide range of tools. Use them wisely.

It can be tempting to run with the next big thing. Sometimes a new innovation is really attractive and we cannot wait to show everybody how clever our new toy is. Do not get carried away. You will almost certainly find that a blend of new innovative channels and more traditional methods will yield the best results. The timing and targeting of change communications will need you to know your channels and your audience in order to deliver the most effective results.

Celebrate success

Don't be modest.

Communicate success to stakeholders in order to demonstrate that we are on the right track. Reporting back on short-term goals will help your staff to see that there is merit in our programme of change and that we are heading in the right direction towards achieving our longer term aspirations. Sharing success will also help generate a positive atmosphere around our change culture and will encourage active participation from colleagues.

Be open and honest

What will we tell them?

If you have to ask then something is wrong. You tell it as it is. Sure, we will encounter barriers to success and we will have failures along the way, but the route to embedding a positive culture around identifying, implementing, adopting and embracing change is a route marked with honest and transparent communications. Such an approach demonstrates to all involved that setbacks and failures are an acceptable part of learning and changing. We will never fail if we take the easy road and do nothing, but we are committed to challenging the future. We accept failure just as we celebrate success.

Beware

Do not become complacent just because something works well. Build on your successes but always strive to improve on what you have already achieved.

5 Starting to Evaluate

Communications are sometimes seen as intangible and hard to evaluate. However, it is essential to do this, to assess its worth to an organization. This chapter introduces methods of evaluation so you can start to show the value that communications bring.

Measuring Effectiveness

It is still amazing how many organizations implement communication strategies in support of projects or business changes, but do not measure the effectiveness of these activities.

It is important to evaluate all activities not just the major campaigns that you run. This will enable you to evaluate the success, or otherwise, of individual components. This makes perfect common sense and is an approach that we will take in relation to many other business processes, but communication campaigns are sometimes, erroneously, judged as just one large piece of work.

We must prove the relative value of each channel and activity in order to accurately calculate their respective value and effectiveness. This thorough approach will help us justify future budget requests and target future spending. We therefore need to capture the effect each activity has had on end user behavior. Failure to do so will see us failing to target future spending for optimum value and impact.

This cycle is:

- Planning

- Invoking

- Evaluating

Using experience

This cycle will see us starting off each campaign or project with a strategy based on previous experience. It will allow us to confidently put together our communications strategy for the project or business change on which we are working and recognition at the outset of the need to evaluate will ensure that we capture all relevant data and information as we proceed. The evaluation itself will feed into our next plan and therefore our knowledge base should grow with each new initiative. This is the path to excellence and will help you gain the trust of your organization and help secure future investment. Ultimately we want to deliver best practice in our approach to communications. It is extremely tempting to complete a piece of work, celebrate what went well, give ourselves a pat on the back and move on. Adherence to the cycle above will deliver positive benefits.

Beware

If you cannot prove the value of a channel of communications then you may lose it.

What is the POINT?

So why aren't we performing the cycle on the previous page now?

We have heard numerous answers to this question down the years. However, the same old responses pop up every time. Have a think about what you think might be stopping us evaluating effectively, or perhaps even evaluating at all. Your answers will probably include a few of these:

- I don't have time

- I don't have the resources

- I can't break the body of work down into individual components

- I can't capture the data needed

- It is unnecessary for the project I'm working on

- What is the point? I've done what I was tasked with doing

Hot tip

Thinking of some of the obstacles to evaluation gives you the opportunity to find some solutions before the issues arise.

Well there is a point if we take a sensible approach to our evaluation. We need to ensure that our evaluation is:

- **Pragmatic** – Do what delivers and what is appropriate

- **Objective** – Be honest in your assessment

- **Included** – An integral part of the strategy. Not an afterthought

- **Necessary** – Do not become frustrated in trying to evaluate absolutely everything

- **Transparent** – Publish your findings to the rest of your organization

Securing Buy-in

Those involved in communications are often faced with a cultural challenge before they can deliver what is required. Many project managers, unfortunately, see the need to communicate effectively as an afterthought – not really part of the task. Therefore capturing what is required from your role can sometimes be extremely difficult. The project manager and his team may well be consumed by the need to "deliver" and your communications are merely the window dressing.

We mentioned in Chapter One how the development of a communications strategy is perhaps best viewed as an art rather than a science. This does not sit too well with the structured approach to project management, such as the PRINCE2 model. It will almost definitely not appeal to the disciplined minds putting together our next IT project for a Helpdesk and you may therefore encounter resistance.

Don't forget

PRINCE2 is a methodology for project management. However, although it can be effective it is also fairly rigid in its approach.

Winning people over

In order to win over all of the required people, and secure involvement at an early stage of the project, you will need to first do the following, using the EDIT model:

- Establish what needs to be evaluated

- Demonstrate how you are going to do this

- Indicate what resources you will require

- Target the outputs to be produced

This approach will show that there is a point in evaluating and that underpinning the art of communications there is a solid foundation based on best practice. This pragmatism and structure is essential when analyzing the return achieved on our investment. This makes evaluation a much more scientific function within our communications arena and this approach will help to secure buy-in from all project stakeholders. Some people like to see a structured, scientific approach and if you can demonstrate this then you are well on the way to getting them on your side.

> This approach will show that there is a point in evaluating

Staying SMART

Let us consider again the campaign we looked at earlier: our intention was to promote a healthy lifestyle among our workforce. We gave a number of reasons why this might benefit our organization. So what was our objective?

- Promote a healthier lifestyle among our staff - Not SMART

- Encourage staff to exercise more - Not SMART

- Encourage staff to follow a healthier diet - Not SMART

We have identified that we want to encourage staff to do the above, but that is not our ultimate objective. Appropriate objectives for this campaign may be:

- To reduce staff sick leave by 20% in next financial year

- To increase the staff satisfaction score in the annual staff survey by 10%

- To increase profits by 10% in the next financial year

We have previously concluded that a healthier workforce will improve our chances of achieving these objectives; therefore we have to put together a campaign aimed at delivering this.

Key Performance Indicators

We may set Key Performance Indicators (KPIs) for the above objectives.

KPIs are used to measure our success against a particular goal. If our objective relates to profitability then we will set KPIs around financial spend and income.

85

Hot tip

Key Performance Indicators are much-loved by directors of finance and project managers. So, if you are trying to win them over this is one way to do it.

...cont'd

In this instance, however, we have determined to support these organizational objectives by helping create a healthier and therefore happier and more committed workforce. Given our campaign there are a number of intermediate results that will help to illustrate whether our communications campaign is performing effectively.

In our example what might these intermediate results be?

- Number of staff taking the healthy option from the staff restaurant menu

- Number of staff taking up discounted gym membership offer

- Number of staff taking part in step initiative

- Volume of threads and posts on dedicated area of staff forum

- Quantity of appointments made as part of the free healthcheck offer

Don't forget

Even if a campaign falls narrowly short of its stated objectives it can still be considered a success if it has delivered some improvements. The next challenge is to see how this can be made even better.

These outtake results will indicate whether staff are engaging with our campaign. We cannot, of course, guarantee that success in each of the above will ultimately lead to achievement of the overall goals, but we can evaluate and tweak our communications strategy in response to the levels of uptake of each.

Techniques of Evaluation

What techniques can we adopt in order to accurately evaluate components of our strategy? The task here is to establish what activities provoked a positive reaction from our staff.

Therefore if local gym membership increased, was this due to:

- The posters advertising a 25% reduction?

- Did the adverts in our staff magazine play a part?

- Did the threads on our staff forum cause interests to be aroused and followed up?

- Was there an increase in staff purchasing the healthy option in the staff restaurant? If so, what persuaded them to do so? Was it price? Perhaps we decided to price this attractively in order to incentivize our staff to make that choice

- Was it, perhaps, peer pressure? Did staff feel uncomfortable going for their regular three course meal while colleagues were taking a light snack or salad?

- Were there any other additional factors that we had not catered for in the first place? Always keep an open mind, apart from the elements for which you have planned

Getting a reaction

This is a social example, but it illustrates how different stimuli can elicit responses and that is what our strategy was all about. We wanted people to react, we achieved that and now we need to know what it was that caused them to react favorably. At the same time, we will be keen also to find out what did not work. Remember, our efforts can cause bad reactions, good reactions or no/neutral reactions. We need to know what worked and what did not so we can prepare better for future communications exercises.

> We need to know what worked and what didn't so we can prepare better for future communications exercises

Beware

Evaluation can be a time-consuming process but it is a vital part of assessing the success of campaigns and the communications designed to promote and publicize them.

87

Becoming Engaged

Different channels require different techniques. Of course, the proliferation of social media tools makes engaging with staff/customers much easier. We can communicate in so many different ways and the evaluation of each of these channels will require differing levels of effort, imagination and technology. Channels also require to be broken down so that we can establish with more pinpoint accuracy just how effective our approach has been:

● **Data** leads to **Information**, which leads to **Knowledge**

So we can engage with staff at face to face meetings; we can chat on-line; we can send out a staff survey. All of this direct interaction will yield very thorough and useful information. However, there are other, more subtle, ways to establish where we were successful and where we fell short.

Measuring success

Think again about the campaign aimed at tackling domestic violence, which was looked at in Chapter Three. Say we placed posters at bus stops encouraging those affected to seek help via our helpline. We can use a number of different lines and position posters geographically so that one particular number relates to a certain area. This could tell us one of two things. If calls to that number are high then the campaign has worked well in that area, through our careful planning about poster location; or, this particular problem is more prevalent in that location. By comparing responses to posters sited in similar locations in each area we can begin to understand whether it was the location of the poster which delivered a higher number of calls or whether the problem is greater in that district.

So when, nowadays, you scan an advertisement with your phone, you can be assured that this particular code will be sending detailed information about the date, time and location of the poster you have scanned. This helps to evaluate the channel in a way which, in the past, would have required more imagination and effort.

In our healthy lifestyle example, the placement of different references for callers to quote in each advertisement promoting a discounted gym membership, will allow this information to be captured and the effectiveness of our efforts to be gauged.

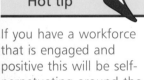

Hot tip

If you have a workforce that is engaged and positive this will be self-perpetuating around the organization. People who are engaged, tend to pass this enthusiasm on to their colleagues who, hopefully, will become more engaged and positive themselves.

Planning for the Future

As stated previously (and it cannot be overstated) such evaluation will help to prove the effectiveness of your communications strategy. In turn this will help you target future campaigns more accurately, but it will play a huge role in securing investment in the channels which work. In a world where budgets are being cut, having the ability to say, "We need to invest a bit more money in our social media tools - here's where they delivered value last year and here's the evidence" is priceless.

When evaluating, it is vitally important to make a clear distinction between the effectiveness of the communications strategy and the success of the project.

Many projects fail to deliver their stated aims. It is a fact of life: projects fail. By the same token, a great many projects do deliver what they set out to deliver. The crucial point to note here is that a failed project does not necessarily mean a bad communications strategy. If we are going to take advantage of that statement then we need to also consider that a great project does not necessarily mean great communications.

> A failed project does not necessarily mean a bad communications strategy

Beware

If a project or campaign is considered to have failed, do not try and apportion blame. Instead, look at what did not work well and ensure that this is addressed before the next project or campaign.

So if our organization discovered that it had failed to deliver the reduction in sick absence and the increase in productivity, our healthy eating campaign may be deemed to have failed also. Of course, it may not have done. It may be that the parallel drawn between a healthy workforce and increased productivity was flawed. It may also be the case that external factors influenced our campaign. The local gym perhaps increased its monthly subscription after a few months, a fantastic fast-food restaurant opened up around the corner and our staff just could not resist!

We need to be aware of, capture and document all external factors which may have an impact on our campaign. Unfortunately, very often after that initial push, many organizations fail to back up their communications strategy and therefore the message becomes diluted and ultimately is lost. Do not forget the cycle of revisiting, tweaking and going again.

Controlling Evaluation

Is it valid to say that the strategy was excellent, but that the mood was negative, the time was wrong or the people just did not want to change? That makes for a good debate, but in our view the answer is no. A good strategy understands and takes into account the culture, it is constructed for the time in which it exists and it reflects our knowledge of our audience.

Therefore you must know and document the risks. Your strategy must be a living and breathing initiative which you revisit regularly in order to ensure that it remains fit for purpose.

Through this approach you will be certain that you are evaluating the strategy in the correct context. You can then evaluate it accurately and gain a true reading of its overall worth and the value of each component.

What and when?

At the very outset of us discussing our approach to a communications strategy we used the analogy of a journey.

Our daily journey to work requires little planning and we instinctively know if it is going well: our bus stops more often than usual or our subway train sits at a stop signal for five minutes. It is actually quite amazing how accurately we can gauge the success or otherwise of our commute.

On my walk to the train station I can tell whether I am running to time by the location of certain people whom I usually encounter on my journey. The day to day is quite straightforward to evaluate.

Being measured

Large scale campaigns, long-term projects and changes with significant impact can require a more structured and measured approach than looking at the elements of our daily commute.

There was no pun intended by the use of 'measured' when discussing evaluation, but it is the perfect word. It suggests the following in terms of our evaluation:

- Calm

- Structured

- Sensible

Don't forget

Do not be afraid to identify any negative issues as a result of evaluation. This is the first step to putting things right.

90

- Objective
- Appropriate
- Level-headed
- Evaluated

If you can deliver measured communications in all senses of the word then you are on target to deliver.

Stages in a campaign

So what stages of awareness will our audience go through during a more lengthy campaign?

1 Initially we are looking for them to be aware that e.g. our Healthy Living campaign exists

2 Then we want them to understand its aims

3 To understand how it may benefit them

4 To feel that there is something in it of interest to them

5 To participate

Note that we can directly influence Steps 1, 2 and 3. However, Steps 4 and 5 are down to the individual. You have put it out there, you have explained what it is about and you have advertised the benefits to be derived. How people feel about what you have told them and what they do about it are out of your control to a certain extent.

Making it attractive

However, if you manage your campaign as effectively and positively as possible then this can also have an influence on Steps 4 and 5. You cannot force people to take part in a campaign, but you can make it appear so attractive and beneficial that they will want to be part of it. This type of participation is the best because it means that people will be approaching it with a positive view.

Hot tip

Even non-business campaigns should be viewed as a positive thing for an organization. For instance, with the example here, a healthier workforce will have fewer sick days and should be more productive.

Return on Investment

The one piece of evaluation that a lot of organizations are good at is value for money. When there is a monetary result we feel pretty confident about measuring what we got back as a result of one of our campaigns.

Sometimes, in fact, all too often, we can be a little bit economical with the facts when it comes to what we have spent. You have probably done it without realizing it, but thankfully things seem to be changing and capturing costs is becoming more structured, perhaps through necessity.

Capturing costs

The key is to capture everything we do and, where possible, attach a cost. This is straightforward enough when we have to pay a bill for the printing of a series of posters. Simple; the printer sends us an invoice, we submit it to our finance section for payment and we register the cost against the particular project and subtract it from our print budget.

What about the cost of the staff member who spent two days designing the poster and three hours meeting with the printer to agree costs and timescales? Internal costs must be captured and allocated accurately, just in the same way that we do with external ones. Again, this provides us with a total cost, a true picture of the amount we must recover if we are to break even on a project that delivers a financial payback.

And remember to include the costs associated with evaluating your campaign! Typically these will account for 7% – 10% of your budget for the strategy on which you are engaged.

The Big Picture

We started this chapter by stating that lots of organizations still do not evaluate their communications campaigns accurately, or in many cases, whatsoever. We gave a number of the common excuses.

Consider where we are now:

- We know where our communications objectives fit in

- We know to set performance indicators

- We recognize the importance of understanding our audience

- We know that we need to plan, invoke, evaluate and then tweak and go again

- We can evaluate component channels

- We know how channels are used

- We know we have to capture all costs

It is clear that we have an enormous amount of valuable information which will contribute to our evaluation plan. We now understand why we have to do it for all strategies.

Benchmarking for evaluation

In this information age, we have a great advantage when it comes to data capture for benchmarking purposes. We are literally one press of a button away from accessing useful information which can also help greatly when it comes to evaluating our campaign.

So, for example, when we wish to judge how successful we were in getting staff to join the local gym, we can easily access information on rates of gym membership in our area. If the average locally is 2% gym membership, our staff had a rate of 1.3% before our campaign and this had increased to 2.2% after our campaign, then we have figures to hand which show that we made a difference and that this difference exceeded what might have been reasonably expected.

Don't forget

Benchmarking is an excellent starting point for future communications campaigns. However, there also needs to be some flexibility as each campaign will be slightly different in approach from previous ones.

93

Post Campaign Review

So we have shown that we can perform evaluations which are:

- Measured

- Meaningful

- Accurate

We can undoubtedly report back on the success of our campaign, but there is one other task which should always be completed.

Obtaining feedback

Go out, one more time, to your audience and ask for their feedback. There will have been aspects of your campaign which

they will have liked and others which will almost certainly have irritated. Sometimes the aspects which irritated might also have been very effective; we always remember a radio jingle that we hated or a TV commercial which we felt had insulted our intelligence. Sometimes this irritating channel can be used quite deliberately in order to grab the attention of the audience. If that was our intention, and it served a purpose, then all well and good.

However, spending some time at the end to get feedback from the audience can be incredibly valuable. It can confirm details of our evaluation or help set the context in which a particular channel or activity proved successful/unsuccessful.

Spending some time at the end to get feedback from our audience can be incredibly valuable

Again, all of this information feeds into our next campaign, helping us target our communications more accurately and reducing startup costs next time round. We have the data which provides the information which leads to the knowledge.

Don't forget

Feedback is only useful if it is acted upon. People have to see the results of the feedback and be made aware of any changes that have occurred as a result of their feedback.

94

6 Slaying Corporate Jargon

Effective communications is not just about what we say, but also about how we say it. This chapter looks at how to avoid corporate jargon and create communications that is clear, concise and meaningful.

Hiding Behind Jargon

If anyone works in the business world they will undoubtedly come across endless examples of corporate jargon, and probably sooner rather than later. Impenetrable documents, convoluted language and the overuse of acronyms, technical words and phrases all contribute to corporate jargon.

For the poor communicator, corporate jargon can be a godsend as it gives them a barrier behind which they can hide. There is a misconception with some communicators that the more complicated a document is, the better it is. However, the opposite is in fact true and those who use corporate jargon break one of the basic rules of communications: everyone should be able to understand what you are saying.

Everyone should be able to understand what you are saying

There is also a certain arrogance about people who use corporate jargon as a means of communication, as if they want to show their expertise, even if their audience is confused as to what they are trying to say. Corporate communications is not a place to try and flaunt your superior knowledge; it is somewhere to try and ensure that the message is produced in a way that is as accessible as possible to everyone in the organization.

Corporate jargon can also be deliberately used in communications to try and hide the real message, by burying it so deeply in long words and technical phrases that it confuses the audience. The problems with this are two-fold. Firstly, the message will still ultimately be the same: if it is hidden within corporate jargon it will just take people longer to get to it. Secondly, if you are seen to be using corporate jargon people will start to doubt your ability as a communicator and mistrust what you do in the future.

What is Corporate Jargon?

The simple definition for corporate jargon is a piece of business writing that is not easily understood because of its complexity. However, there are a few specific items that make up corporate jargon:

- The overuse of technical or specialized terms or phrases. Every business organization has its fair share of words and phrases that are specific to its own work, but, if possible, these should be kept to a minimum in corporate communications. If you do have to use technical phrases, make sure that they are properly explained in the context of the document. Also, remember that newer people in the organization may not be as familiar with all of its specialized words and phrases

- Complex language and vocabulary. Corporate communications should not be an excuse to show off your mastery of the English language and your huge vocabulary. Think about your audience and tailor your writing accordingly

- Unexplained use of acronyms. Acronyms can be another major contributor to corporate jargon. Sentences such as, 'The IMT of the HHR makes the IPT less than the QSO' can leave even the most experienced person in an organization scratching  their head as to what it all means. As with technical phrases, acronyms are sometimes unavoidable and they can provide a useful shortcut for writing down long phrases. However, always ask yourself if everyone in your audience will understand a certain acronym. If not, write it out in full and, if necessary, explain what it means. In general, the rule for acronyms is to spell them out the first time they are used and then the acronym can be used on its own e.g. Return on Investment (ROI) and then as ROI

- Long-winded sentences and paragraphs. Sometimes, when people feel they have a lot to say, they let it all tumble out in long sentences and paragraphs, barely pausing for breath. This can cause the reader to forget what was being said at the beginning of the sentence. As a general rule, write one sentence for each idea and keep paragraphs to a maximum of about ten sentences

Hot tip

Keep a glossary of technical terms and phrases and publish this on the corporate intranet so that people can refer to it if required.

Don't forget

Essentially, corporate jargon is really just bad writing i.e. it does not convey the message it is meant to.

Reading Age and Readability

In order to cut through corporate jargon and start writing clear, effective and readable documents, it is important to first understand two concepts:

- Reading age

- Readability

Reading age

The term reading age refers to someone's reading ability in relation to an average age at which this level is generally found. This is usually in terms of a child's age. The reason for this is that most people reach their full reading age by about age of 16, even if their reading age is above 16.

The importance of reading age in terms of corporate communications is that you should know how to create your documents at an appropriate reading age level for your audience. This means that it should not be pitched at a very low level, but equally, it should not be at the top end of the scale either.

Create your documents at an appropriate reading age level for your audience

There are different methods for measuring reading age and different calculations for various types of publications. As an approximation, the reading age of various items are:

- The average reading age of the UK population is 9 years

- The reading age of a tabloid newspaper is 8-12 years

- The reading age of a broadsheet newspaper is 13-17 years

In terms of this, when creating corporate communications you should aim for a reading age for your documents and websites of between 12-16. However, it is important to know your audience in terms of the types of documents with which they will feel comfortable. Depending on the method of calculation (see next page) the reading age may be more, or less, than the ones here, but, if in doubt, aim for a lower rather than a higher level.

Don't forget

Most workforces contain a diverse range of people, covering tabloid newspaper readers and broadsheet ones. You will have to consider this when you are creating communication documents and try and reach a level that is acceptable to everyone.

Readability

There are a number of factors that influence the readability of a document, including:

- Length of sentences

- Length of words

- Types of words

- Design

- Use of white space

In terms of calculating the reading age of a document, this is done primarily according to word and sentence length. There are several methods that can be used to calculate reading age and some of them are:

- The Gunning Fog Index

- Kincaid Formula

- Flesh Reading Easy Formula

- SMOG-Grading

Each of these methods calculate the readability of a document slightly differently, but this example for the Gunning Fog Index is reasonably representative:

- Select an example of at least 100 words

- Work out the average number of words per sentence

- Count the number of words with three syllables or more (defined as long words)

- Add the average number of words per sentence to the number of words with three syllables of more

- Divide the result by five

- Add five to get the final reading age for the example

Don't forget

The Gunning Fog Index was developed by Robert Gunning, an American businessman, in 1952. Its original aim was to assess text in terms of its readability for US high school students.

Beware

Readability methods do not necessarily guarantee a clear and concise document. Always check things yourself to make sure that you have not used unnecessarily long words or jargon and that sentences are of a reasonable length.

Writing for Readability

Using one of the methods for determining the reading age of a piece of text it is possible to start looking at your corporate writing to see how it can be made easier to read and understand.

Examples for readability

Look at these two examples to see how they differ in terms of readability and how easy they are to understand.

> The gentleman exited his place of residence and perambulated down the boulevard with great alacrity, transporting an exquisite timepiece which was encrusted with priceless and transfixing diamonds. Shortly after his departure he encountered an acquaintance who was known for her loquacious nature: he tried to extricate himself from the situation but his acquaintance was tenacious and insisted on detaining him for an inordinate amount of time, much to his indignation as he had an essential assignation to attend in order to attempt to dispose of his timepiece in return for an enormous consideration.

> The man left his house and walked quickly down the road. He was carrying a sparkling diamond watch. Just after he left, he met a talkative friend of his. He tried to leave but his friend was keen to chat and kept him there for a long time. The man was annoyed, as he had to meet someone to try and sell his watch.

Hot tip

There is a function within Word for checking readability. To do this, access the Spelling and Grammar function, and check on the 'Check grammar with spelling' and 'Show readability statistics' boxes. Then select the text you want to check and select the Spelling and Grammar option.

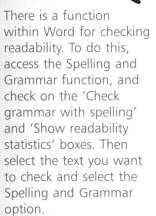

Although these are extreme examples, they illustrate the point about readability. The first example has a reading age of approximately 20, while the second one has a reading age of approximately nine. Therefore, most of the population could understand the second example while only a very small percentage could fully understand the first example. The following areas should be considered when trying to reduce reading age:

- Use shorter sentences. In the first example there are only two sentences, of 27 and 67 words, averaging 47 words per sentence. In the second example the average words per sentence is just below 13. This makes it easier to read, as there is not as much information to process in each sentence. In general, try and keep one idea per sentence. However, this does mean that you have to 'dumb down' your writing to the level of a kindergarten or nursery class

- Use punctuation and parentheses. Even when you are mindful of keeping sentences short, it is always important to remember punctuation. This can help break up sentences and enable you to use slightly longer ones, if required, while still maintaining readability (although punctuation is not usually included in methods of measuring readability). Use a colon to introduce items of a list or an explanation of a preceding clause that can also stand on its own. Use a semi-colon to separate list items or two closely related clauses. Use brackets to include additional information to the main sentence. Also, do not forget the humble comma, which is an excellent way to break up sentences and allow the reader to draw breath

Do not forget the humble comma

- Use shorter and simpler words. Corporate writing should not be an excuse for people to try and show off their vast vocabulary. If people cannot understand what you are saying then you are failing in your role as a communicator. You may like the fact that you know what loquacious means, but your audience will probably much prefer if you say talkative, or chatty, as an alternative. When you are creating corporate documents, look at all of the longer words that you are using and see if there is a more suitable alternative. This may not always be the case, but it is worth checking

Beware

Just because one word is longer than another, do not presume it is more complicated. This is usually the case but not always, so do not discard words purely based on their length.

Designing for Readability

Using clear and understandable language is not the only factor in creating readable documents. The design of documents can also have a significant impact on how easy people find to read them. Some elements of this are:

- Design features
- Color
- Designing for dyslexia
- Fonts
- Letter case
- Line spacing
- White space
- Sub-headings and lists

Don't forget

Unless design is done by an external company, it frequently falls to the person considered to have the best aptitude for it. This means that it is always a good idea to have a basic knowledge of design issues, in case it falls to you.

Design features

It is human nature to try and make things look as nice as possible and it is no different when creating corporate communications documents, either in hard copy or online. Frequently, people may ask you to produce a report, or a website, and give you the instruction, 'Just make it look jazzy'. This usually means that they want some fancy piece of design to help catch the eye. While good design can achieve this the opposite is also true; bad design can have a negative effect on how readers perceive a piece of writing. In general, the 'less is more' rule is a good one to follow in terms of design. The design should add to the document rather than act as a distraction.

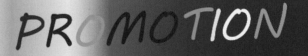

The main area for design features in a document is in headings and header and footer areas. Some points to consider are:

- If you are using text as part of a design feature, make sure that it is legible and that there is a good contrast between the text and the background

- Do not turn text on its side or at different angles - the easiest way to read text is in the normal, traditional, horizontal way, despite what designers may think

- Limit the number of colors in the design. Two or three at the most is ideal. More than this and the design will become distracting or irritating

Color

The use of color is not only an issue in terms of design elements in a document. It is also a factor in terms of text and background. One way in which design can enhance a document or website is to change the color of the text and/or the background. While this can sometimes be effective, there is also a risk of making the text less legible. For instance, light blue text on a gray background will not provide a suitable contrast, while pink text on a bright orange background will probably give the reader a headache, sooner rather than later.

For instance, light blue text on a gray background will not provide a suitable contrast, while pink text on a bright orange background will probably give the reader a headache, sooner rather than later.

Don't forget

Although it may be considered a bit boring in some design circles, black on white is still one of the most effective combinations for text.

103

Designing for dyslexia

One area where the issue of color is very important is in dealing with dyslexia.

Dyslexia means having difficulty with words and it affects approximately 10% of the population (British Dyslexia Association). Therefore, it is essential to ensure that this proportion of the workforce are catered for when designing workplace communications, whenever possible. The first step is to recognize that dyslexia is a significant problem in terms of communication. Also, there may be a significant number of people who are not fully aware that they have dyslexia, or do not want to draw this to people's attention.

There are a range of issues concerned with dyslexia in the workplace, but in terms of communications there are a number of areas that can be looked at:

● For written material, allow for extra time to read and understand the information

● People with dyslexia frequently have difficulty with certain colored backgrounds for text. Black text on a white background is not always the best option: black on a pale yellow background is often the best combination for people with dyslexia, for both hard copy and computer screens

Don't forget

Anyone concerned about dyslexia in the workplace should initially speak to their HR department or a welfare officer. These conversations should be treated in confidence.

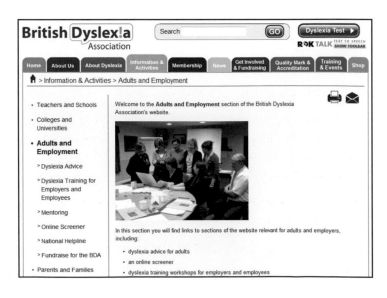

- Provide the means to change the background color of computer screens

- Investigate the use of assistive technology for reading from computer screens. This is usually in the form of software that reads what is on the screen, rather than the user having to read it for themselves. There is also assistive technology software that can be used for tasks such as mindmapping

- Be prepared to look at alternatives to providing written communications. This could be in the form of face to face, video, audio descriptions and also diagrams and charts. If someone is struggling with written text they should not be penalized for this and they should be given the same opportunities as everyone else in terms of receiving and consuming corporate communications

> **Be prepared to look at alternatives to providing written communications**

Beware

When dealing with any type of technology to assist with dyslexia always speak to the individuals involved first. Do this in confidence, to ensure that they are comfortable using this type of assistance in the workplace, in front of their colleagues.

- Check to ensure that the most important points in a document have been fully understood. However, do this in a sympathetic way, preferably in private, so as not cause any embarrassment or awkwardness

- Reading on a computer screen can be particularly tiring and difficult so provide an anti-glare filter and ensure that people get regular breaks from screen work. Alternate this with tasks that do not require reading (this should be done for everyone, if possible, not just people with dyslexia)

- Do not ask people with dyslexia to perform any tasks that may put them in an awkward situation, such as taking the minutes of a meeting or asking them to do a written presentation on a flipchart or smartboard

Two very useful websites to look at for a wealth of information and resources about dyslexia are:

- The International Dyslexia Association at www.interdys.org

- The British Dyslexia Association at www.bdadyslexia.org.uk

...cont'd

White space

One of the most important elements of design for communication documents is something that is blank. The white space around text is essential in ensuring that it is inviting to look at and make people want to start reading. It is also beneficial when text is being read: it is more relaxing to read something if there is a sufficient amount of white space, rather than having text that is very tightly packed together.

There are a number of ways in which white space can be incorporated into a piece of text, whether it is a hard copy document or on a website:

White space around text is essential in ensuring that it is inviting to look at and makes people want to start reading

Don't forget

The term 'leading' comes from the printing industry from the days when pieces of lead were used to separate lines of text in a printing press.

- Margins and headers and footers. Make sure that these are generous enough so that the text is not tight up against any edges of the page, or screen

- Line spacing. This is the amount of spacing between lines of text and is known as leading. Word processors usually apply an automatic amount of leading, based on the font size being used. However, this can be changed to specific amounts and it is worth experimenting with the leading to see the effect it has on the layout of the text

- Lists. Numbered and bulleted lists are an excellent option for increasing the amount of white space in a document. They are also effective in breaking up the text and presenting specific pieces of information

- Sub-headings. This is another useful device for creating white space and also giving the reader an indication of what is coming next in a document

The examples on the opposite page show the difference between a page of text with sufficient white space, with elements such as sub-headings and lists, and one with tightly packed text.

White space
One of the most important elements of design for communications documents is something that is blank. The white space around text is essential to ensuring that it is inviting to look at and make people want to start reading. It is also benefical when text is being read: it is more relaxing to read something if there is a sufficient amount of white space, rather than having text that is very tightly packed together and therefore harder to read.
There are a number of ways in which white space can be incorporated into a piece of text, whether it is a hard copy document or on a website: (the theory is pretty much the same for both).
Margins and headers and footers. Make sure that these are generous enough so that the text is not tight up against any edges of the page, or screen. If not, it will be much harder to read.
Line spacing. This is the amount of spacing between lines of text and is known as leading. Word processors usually apply an automatic amount of leading, based on the font size being used. However, this can be changed to specific amounts and it is worth experimenting with the leading to see the effect it has on the layout of the text. A higher level of leading gives more space.
Lists. Numbered and bulleted lists are an excellent options for increasing the amount of white space in a document. They are also effective in breaking up the text and presenting specific piece of information in a more engaging way.
Sub-headings. This is another useful device for creating white space and also giving the reader an indication of what is coming next in a document i.e. using it as a road sign to the next item
The examples on the opposite page show the difference between a page of text with sufficient white space, and elements such as sub-headings and lists, and one with tightly packed text.

Don't forget

Another way to create white space is to ensure there is a line space between paragraphs.

107

White space
One of the most important elements of design for communications documents is something that is blank. The white space around text is essential to ensuring that it is inviting to look at and make people want to start reading. It is also benefical when text is being read: it is more relaxing to read something if there is a sufficient amount of white space, rather than having text that is very tightly packed together.

There are a number of ways in which white space can be incorporated into a piece of text, whether it is a hard copy document or on a website:

- Margins and headers and footers. Make sure that these are generous enough so that the text is not tight up against any edges of the page, or screen

- Line spacing. This is the amount of spacing between lines of text and is known as leading. Word processors usually apply an automatic amount of leading, based on the font size being used. However, this can be changed to specific amounts and it is worth experimenting with the leading to see the effect it has on the layout of the text

Lists and subheadings
- Lists. Numbered and bulleted lists are an excellent options for increasing the amount of white space in a document. They are also effective in breaking up the text and presenting specific piece of information

- Sub-headings. This is another useful device for creating white space and also giving the reader an indication of what is coming next in a document

The examples on the opposite page show the difference between a page of text with sufficient white space, and elements such as sub-headings and lists, and one with tightly packed text.

Hot tip

Use color for headings, sub-headings and bullet points, for emphasis and to add an extra design element to a document.

...cont'd

Fonts

A font is a typography term describing the characteristics of a particular typeface. This is usually in relation to the size and name of a typeface e.g. 11-point Arial. A font family also includes the variation of the typeface in terms of items such as bold and italics e.g. 10-point Helvetica Bold.

Two other terms that are used in relation to fonts are serif and sans serif. These refers to the loops, or lack of, on individual letters in a font family. Serif fonts are those that have loops at the ends of letters while sans serif fonts do not. An example of a serif font is TimesNewRoman and an example of a sans serif font is Arial.

In terms of using fonts in publications the following rules are generally followed:

● Use serif fonts for printed material

● Use sans serif fonts for text on computer screens

Don't forget

Experiment with different fonts, rather than just the widely-used TimesNewRoman and Arial options.

> Use serif fonts for printed material
>
> Use sans serif fonts for text on computer screens

Letter case

Whether letters are written in upper or lower case can have an impact on how easy it is to read text. There is sometimes the perception that words in uppercase are easier to read and more effective for emphasis. In fact, the opposite is true: it is easier to read words in mixed case because our minds work by assessing the shape of a word as well as the letters used. Since mixed case has ascenders and descenders this provides more of a contrast, as opposed to the more block-like shape of words in uppercase.

> TEXT IN CAPS CAN BE HARDER TO READ
>
> Than text that has a mix of upper and lowercase

Using Plain English

The Plain English Campaign was formed in 1979 and is a independent body dedicated to the use of clear English in public communications. One of the aims of the campaign is for the creation of crystal clear communications in public documents and to ensure that the right message is being given, in the right way, to the right audience. This is done in a number of ways:

- Courses. The Plain English Campaign holds a number of different training courses including in-house, online and open courses. The courses cover subjects including business writing, writing for websites, grammar and report writing

- Guides. A range of guides can be downloaded from the Plain English Campaign website at www.plainenglish.co.uk. The website also contains a range of resource material for removing gobbledygook, jargon and legalese

Don't forget

Using Plain English does not mean 'dumbing down' your writing. There is nothing wrong with retaining your own style while still trying to make everything as clear as possible

- Awards. There is an annual Plain English Campaign awards ceremony, covering communications from all walks of public life. There are also Crystal Mark awards which are given as a mark of approval for documents that are written with a sufficient level of clarity. Crystal Mark awards have to be applied for and there are versions for hard copy and Web documents and writing

Guidelines and Training

Good communications do not happen by accident and it is something that has to be worked at constantly and continually. In terms of producing good written communications, one robust way to do this is to create a Guide to Written Communications, to which everyone should have access.

What to include

A Guide to Written Communications should provide information so that everyone in the organization can understand why things are written in the way they are and also be able to produce effective written work themselves. If everyone follows the Guide to Written Communications then a consistent corporate style should be created throughout the organization.

Some items that should be included in a Guide to Written Communications are:

- Grammar. This can sometimes be the lost element in written communications. The days of grammar being taught in great detail in schools seems to have become a thing of the past. However, good grammar should not be taken for granted and it is something that can damage the impact of a document if it is ignored. People rarely congratulate you for good grammar, but they will quickly spot bad grammar. There are a lot of books and courses that deal with grammar in corporate communications and these are always a good investment

- Punctuation. Include information about punctuation such as the use of commas, colons, semi-colons, quotation marks, apostrophes, question marks and exclamation marks. If you are including information about grammar, this is also a good place to include information about punctuation

- Word use. Stress the need to use words that people can understand rather showing off your own vocabulary. Usually shorter words are better than longer ones, but it is important to use words that are appropriate to what you are saying

- Document length. When creating a Guide to Written Communications you can practice what you preach and create a concise document that delivers the information that is needed, without any unnecessary additional material. Stress that it is the content that counts, rather than the length of the document.

- Sentence length. As with document length, sentence length should be flagged up, to be kept to a reasonable length. In general, keep one idea to one sentence

- Commonly misspelled words. We all have our own pet dislikes about words that are commonly misspelled. With spell checkers in word processing programs this can be less of an issue, but there is still the chance of words being misused, such as 'their' and 'there', 'where' and 'were' etc. It is still important to proofread documents to ensure that spelling is correct. One particular error to look out for is the use of 'its'. This only ever has an apostrophe as a contraction for 'it is' (or 'it has'). 'Its' is a possessive noun i.e. referring to something that belongs to someone or something

- Active voice. This refers to when the subject in a sentence is the doer of an action. This is generally perceived as being a more positive type of writing than using the passive voice, where the subject has the action done to it. 'The boy kicked the ball' is active, while 'The ball was kicked by the boy' is passive

- Design. The design features on the previous pages should also be considered in any guidelines and it should be acknowledged that design is an important part of creating documents that are easier to read

Training

Once a Guide to Written Communications has been created, that is only some of the work done. You also have to ensure that the people who are primarily concerned with creating written

communications have suitable training so they can feel comfortable in their roles. This is true whether they are working directly in communications, or if they regularly produce written work as part of their own roles.

Training should be done on a face to face basis, so that discussions can take place and real life examples can be used. This type of training can be done internally or with external providers.

Beware

Another common error occurs with the use of 'your' rather than 'you're' as a contraction of 'you are'. This is creeping into common usage more now as a result of its use in text messages and tweets.

Hot tip

If possible, always get someone else to proofread your work. It is always easier to check what other people have written; with your own work you sometimes think you know what you have written and do not see mistakes.

Corporate Jargon Bingo

Although it is just for fun in some ways, Corporate Jargon Bingo (also known as Buzzword Bingo and other, less complimentary, phrases) can be useful in flagging up the use of jargon within an organization. The point of this is to create a list of jargon and then tick items off when they are used in spoken, or written, communications.

Corporate Jargon Bingo usually involves the speaker or writer of the work not knowing what is being done and, in this respect, it can sometimes be a questionable activity. However, if it is then brought up in a proper and reasonable fashion it could be used to address the issue of corporate jargon. Some items to watch for are:

- Benchmarking
- Blue-sky thinking
- Business process reengineering
- Customer-centric
- Empowerment
- Incentivize
- Implementation
- Leverage
- Paradigm shift
- Proactive
- Scalable
- Strategize
- Synergy
- Thinking outside the box
- Touch base
- Touchpoint
- User-centric
- Working in silos

Beware

Most of us are prone to falling into the trap of using corporate jargon from time to time, so do not be too critical of other people as it may come back to haunt you.

7 Creating Websites That Work

In the world of modern communications, websites are at the heart of most of what we do. This chapter looks at ensuring that both internal and external websites are as well designed as possible and it also shows how to make sure that the content on the sites is as engaging as possible.

Defining Your Web Audience

Before you think about creating, or revising, a website you should think about who your audience is and what it is you want to say to them. There is little point in having a beautifully designed website if you are targeting the content at the wrong people.

Internal audience

By definition your internal and external audiences will be different. Internally your website will be an intranet, to provide information to staff, but not externally. Generally, this will be a mixed audience but one area you should look at is the age of your workforce. This can roughly be divided up into the following:

- Baby Boomers
- Generation X
- Generation Y

Baby Boomers

The term 'Baby Boomers' is given to the group of people born in an approximate 20 year period following World War II. Baby Boomers grew up wanting to have an improved society and lived through the radical cultural changes of the 1960s. This has led to the theory that Baby Boomers rejected traditional values. However, as they grew older and became involved with their own families and a working life, this does not seem to be fully borne out.

In terms of the workplace Baby Boomers are still a fairly traditional group: they are happy to be defined by their job and they see it as something that is an important part of their identity. The Baby Boomers are probably the last generation to embrace the concept of a 'job for life' i.e. one job that they would work in continually until they retired.

Hot tip
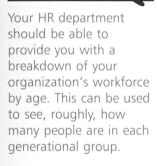

Your HR department should be able to provide you with a breakdown of your organization's workforce by age. This can be used to see, roughly, how many people are in each generational group.

Generation X

The Generation X (sometimes also known as Gen X) is the one that came after the Baby Boomers. The timescale for this is being born approximately from the mid 1960s to the mid 1980s.

The key word in relation to Generation X is change. They are not prepared to sit back and put up with things that they do not like. This is not necessarily a sign of impatience, but rather an understanding that there are other options out there. They are not scared of change and embrace it as a positive thing.

In terms of communicating with Generation X, they want their information in a variety of formats and in as a straightforward way as possible. They will not tolerate being patronized or having to deal with what they see as waffle or jargon.

Hot tip

It is a good idea to have people from the different generational groups on your communications team. This will ensure that all different perspectives are taken into consideration.

Generation Y

Also, known as the Net Generation, Generation Y is an extension of Generation X. They have grown up with the Web, text and social media and expect things to happen immediately, if not sooner. They can be fairly fickle and if they do not like something then they will quickly move on to something else. Also, they are at ease with multitasking and will happily consume communications from different channels at the same time.

...cont'd

External Audience

The type of external website your organization has, and therefore its potential target audience, will depend on your type of business. In general though, your website will be a window for displaying the goods and services that you offer. The types of groups that you could be aiming your website at are:

- Business community. Most professional websites are aimed at some part of the business community. Therefore, in terms of design, it is important to make your website look efficient and business-like. Look at other business websites to see the types of features that they use. This does not mean your website has to be dull or uninspiring, but it should be clear at first sight that people are looking at a business website

- Specific customer groups. If you are selling specific goods or services then you will want to target the customers who are interested in this type of product. For instance, if you manufacture medical supplies then you will be interested in reaching people in this profession, so your website will be designed with this in mind

- General public. For public services, the main consumers of information on an external website are usually the general public. This is a more diverse group than with specific business groups. In terms of design you will have to think about the different generational groups. Depending on your business you may be able to target one or another, but if you are dealing with them all then your design and content will have to take this into consideration

Don't forget

In terms of design, your external site and your intranet should have the same corporate look and feel, but retain their own individual identities.

Dealing With Generations

Understanding the demographic of your workforce in terms of generational differences is important in terms of how you present your communications. For instance, a Baby Boomer may conscientiously read through something on the intranet, even if they are not very interested in it, as they believe that this is what you should do when you are at work. However, for Generation X and Y, if you do not capture their interest in the first few minutes (or, more likely, seconds) then they will quickly move on to texting their friends or checking their Facebook pages.

If there is a larger number of older or younger people this could have an impact in the following areas:

- Computer literacy. Although Baby Boomers frequently have excellent computer skills they do not always have the intuitive understanding of the younger generation who have grown up with computers and use them as second nature. They tend to not need, or want, to have things explained to them but would rather experiment and find things out for themselves. Do not be surprised if the Generation Xs and Ys prefer to sit and try things out rather than be told what to do

- Social media. This is something that it part of the daily DNA of the Generation Xs and Ys. Life without texting, Facebook or Twitter may seem unimaginable and they often view this as their main form of communications. By comparison even email can be seen as old fashioned and cumbersome. This should be acknowledged in the design of the intranet and, if possible, elements of social media sites should be incorporated into it

- Design. The aim of all Web design should be to be as clear and as accessible as possible. However, Baby Boomers may feel more comfortable with a traditional type of design, where the navigation is clear and the content is presented in a straightforward way. Generation Xs and Ys may prefer something with a more dynamic design with additional features, in order to keep their attention

- Content. Regardless of your audience, you should always aim to keep your content as engaging as possible. However, you may have less time to catch the attention of the Generation Xs and Ys than you do for Baby Boomers

Hot tip

If you are introducing new communication technologies, such as social media elements on your intranet, offer training for everyone who wants it so that they feel involved and can use the technologies to their maximum potential and impact.

How Websites Differ

Although intranets and external sites are similar in terms of both being websites from the same organization, they are very different in terms of their role and function. They should be viewed as two different entities, even though they could be produced from the same Web publishing system or Content Management System.

Intranets

In many organizations the intranet will be the primary source of internal communications. It is therefore essential that it is implemented and managed correctly. Four important points to remember about an intranet are:

- It should be seen as a tool for the staff, rather than senior management. The workforce needs to feel a sense of ownership with an intranet and if they think it is just being used as a propaganda tool for senior management then they will quickly start to avoid it, or worse, distrust it

- It is functional. Ideally people should look up the intranet at least on a daily basis. This is usually to get the latest news updates, or to look for background information on something. Therefore they do not want to spend time looking at the latest whizz-bang Web effects; they just want to find the information that they want and then get on with something else. This is not to say that the design  cannot be engaging, but after a while the users will no longer be conscious about the design, unless it hinders them in finding what they want

- It is not all corporate. Despite what managers may think, or wish for, people do not want to spend their whole working day consuming corporate information. Social content should be viewed as something to encourage people to use the intranet and the hope is that they will then view it as a comprehensive information service covering a range of subjects (see page 132 for more details)

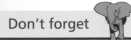

Don't forget

There can sometimes be a battle for the control of the intranet, but it is first and foremost a communications tool and so should be managed by the communications team. They should also be responsible for the content, or at least producing guidelines for adding content.

- It is about the people. At the end of the day, the intranet users are people and they should be viewed as such, rather than corporate robots. If you always keep this in mind when you are creating content then it should have more of a human touch rather than a corporate vehicle. This does not mean that you should start scattering jokes all over the intranet, but don't be afraid to include a bit of personality in the content - think of it as real content for real people

External websites

The most obvious difference about an external website to an intranet is that it is available to anyone with an Internet connection. This has implications for both the content and design of an external website:

- Catching attention. Unlike with the intranet, you do not have a captive audience for your website. There is a lot of competition for people's attention on the Web and if they access your site you will only have a few seconds to catch their attention and make them stay there (according to some calculations people decide within the first 17 seconds whether to stay on a website, although others put it as low as six seconds). Therefore your design has to be engaging and the overall look of the site inviting in terms of appearance and navigation. As with a lot of things in life, you do not get the chance to make a second impression on the Web

You do not get the chance to make a second impression on the Web

- Make it clear where to go. After the initial impression, most visitors to websites what to know how to navigate around. At the same time, they do not want to spend a lot of time trying to work this out. Make sure that your navigation is clear and obvious: this is not an area to try and be too subtle or clever (see pages 120–125 for details about website navigation)

- Search results. One of the best ways to get users to your external website is through results from a search engine such as Google. One way to do this is to have a robust process for including metadata (see pages 127–129 for searching details)

Beware

If you include links on your website that go to other sites, your audience may leave your site via these links and not come back.

Navigation That Works

When looking at the design of a website, one of the most essential elements is the navigation: if there is not a clear way for people to get around a site they will not waste much of their time trying to succeed. The issues regarding navigation are the same for intranets and external websites.

There are a number of elements that can be looked at in relation to navigation:

- Main navigation
- Secondary navigation
- Buttons and Menus
- Breadcrumb trails
- Home buttons
- Anchors
- Hyperlinks
- Site Map

Main navigation

The main navigation of a website is usually a collection of buttons that provide access to the top level categories of the site e.g. About Us, News, Our Products, Our Services, Contact Us. The buttons can be created individually or, as is now more common, they can be included within a navigation bar. The standard position for a main navigation bar is along the top of the website and this should appear in this position on every page of the site.

Hot tip

When you access an item in the main navigation (or any other navigation bars) this can be highlighted with a different color to indicate to the user where they are on the site.

Secondary navigation

The items in your secondary navigation are those in each of the main categories in the main navigation. So if there are ten items within the Our Products category, then these will become the secondary navigation.

As with main navigation, secondary navigation is usually created as a navigation bar. This can be located under the main navigation bar at the top of the screen

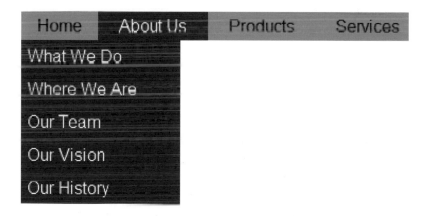

or down the side of the screen.

Don't forget

If you have levels in the secondary section, you can use two top navigation bars and one side navigation bar.

When an another item is selected in the main navigation, the secondary navigation bar changes to reflect the required items e.g when the Products button is clicked on the main navigation the available Products sections are shown in the secondary navigation.

When you click on an item of secondary navigation you will go to that item in a site structure e.g. if you click on Printers you will go to that page within the Products section. It should be clearly indicated to the user where they are in the site. This can be done with a breadcrumb trail (see page 123).

...cont'd

Buttons and Menus

The items that make up navigation bars are buttons and menus. These can be individual graphical elements, or created as one graphical element with the button functionality then added to relevant areas. Buttons can be made to change appearance when they are accessed, so the user knows where they are on the site. This is known as a rollover button and can be in form of the background changing color or the text changing color. More dramatic rollover effects can also be produced, but the ones here are most suitable for business websites.

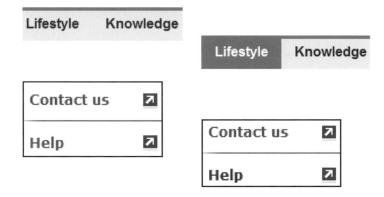

Beware

Rollover menus are much-loved by Web designers, but always check with your users to see what their views about them are.

Rollover menus can also be created. This is where the secondary navigation appears as an extension of the menu button, when it is clicked on, or the cursor is moved over it.

Rollover menus are a useful way to save space on a website and they can look slick from a design point of view. However, some Web browsers do not always render the code correctly for rollover menus. Also, some users find them irritating, particularly if the rollover menu disappears before they have the chance to click on an item, as can happen.

Breadcrumb trail

Depending on the number of levels you have on your website (how many pages that a user has to click through to get to the item they want) users may feel they are getting lost in the site and do not know how to get back from where they came. One solution to this is to incorporate a breadcrumb trail into your navigation. This is a list of the pages that the user has navigated through and usually appears at the top of the page, underneath the top navigation bar. As the user moves through different pages, so another item is added to the breadcrumb trail. To move back to previously visited pages the user can click on the items in the breadcrumb trail.

Hot tip

Breadcrumb trails can be created automatically by a lot of Content Management Systems.

123

Good Format

Home>writing for the Web>Roadmap>Good Format

Previous Page | Next Page

When users read Web pages they do so by scanning the page to find pieces of information that are meaningful or useful.

Because of this it is **important** to create a visual roadmap that users can follow when they initially look at a Web page.

Home button

If users should get lost within a website, there should always be the means to get straight back to the homepage in one click. This can be done with a Home button on the main navigation bar and a home link can also be included within any design elements within the main navigation, usually a company logo. If these items are in the main navigation bar they should then appear on all pages within the site.

...cont'd

Anchor points

Anchor points, also known as bookmarks, are used for two main reasons on websites:

- To create links to specific points on a Web page (rather than just opening up a page at the beginning)

- Create functionality for navigating long lists of items

Anchor points work by inserting an anchor (created with a piece of HTML code) at a certain point on a page. A hyperlink is then created which takes the user to the anchor point, wherever it appears on the destination page.

Because of this it is important to create a **visual roadmap** that users can follow when they initially look at a Web page.

Anchor points

Anchor points are used to go to a specific point on a page, rather than opening the page at the top. They are also a good way of navigating around long lists on a page.

Additional links:

See examples of poor format

Read more about visual roadmaps

Anchor points can also be used on items such as alphabetical lists. Anchors points can be inserted at each heading throughout the list and a menu can be created at the top that has links to each anchor point, frequently a letter of the alphabet.

Staff Handbook

Click on a letter below to go to that section of the Staff Handbook.

A | B | C | D | E | F | G | H | I | J | K | L | M | N | O |
P | Q | R | S | T | U | V | W | X | Y | Z

Hot tip

If you have a long list that is accessed via anchor points, make sure that you also include a 'Back to Top' link next to each anchor point. This will enable the user to jump quickly back to the top of the list.

Hyperlinks

The items that link text and images to other web content are known as hyperlinks. Traditionally, for text, hyperlinks appeared with underlining, to indicate the fact a link was present. However, as Web design has become more sophisticated, links are now more commonly created as rollovers i.e. they change appearance when the cursor is passed over them. This can be a change of color or the link appears underlined, but only when the cursor is passed over it.

Beware

In general, it is best not to use underlined text within content on a website, in case the user thinks it indicates a link.

Site Map

A site map is a list of all of the pages within a website and links to each of them. It is an excellent device to enable users to find items on your website and see all of your content on one page. Site maps can be created as text links to all of your pages (typically with the page title as the link) or a graphical representation of the site as a hierarchical diagram.

Don't forget

Hyperlinks can also be created to email addresses rather than Web pages

Site Map

Click on the links below to go to those pages of our site.

A

About Us

Around the Office

Associates

B

Booking Form

Buying From Us

C

Customer Promise

Customer Recommendations

Creating a Taxonomy

Taxonomy in terms of a website just means the way that things are organized. Its official definition is the science of identifying and naming different species and then classifying them into groups. In terms of a Web taxonomy the process is similar:

- Identifying different categories of information

- Grouping the items on your websites into the different categories

Once the taxonomy has been established this is used for the basis of the navigation for the site: the main categories form the main navigation and then the items within these categories form the subsequent navigation and content.

Card sorting

It is perfectly possible to create a taxonomy for both intranets and external sites by using your own knowledge of your organization and your own judgement. However, a more robust method is to consult with the people who are going to be using the site and ask them which categories of information that they think should be included. This can be done with a series of focus groups. This will be easier for an intranet taxonomy as you have a captive audience in relation to this. For an external website it could be more of a challenge; you could ask for volunteers via your existing website, or use an online survey to gather feedback.

One way to create a taxonomy with a focus group is to use a card sorting exercise. To do this:

- Ask people to write down the main headings that they think should be on the site e.g. What We Do, Departments etc.

- Group these together so that you have between 6-10 main headings

- Ask people to write down all of the items that they access on the website

- Match the items of content with an appropriate main heading

- Repeat the exercise with a number of different groups to reach as much of a consensus as possible

Don't forget

When organizing focus groups for creating a taxonomy make sure that you include a range of ages and positions throughout your organization. Everyone will have their own ideas about what is important to have on a website so you need to get as diverse a range of opinions as possible.

Beware

However robust a process you follow for creating a taxonomy you will never make everyone happy. But if you consult as widely as possible then you should be able to meet the needs of the majority of people.

Searching Effectively

One of the most common ways of looking for information on a website is through a search engine. This can either be one for finding something on the Web (such as Google) or a search engine on an individual site which is used to find items on that site. When creating and managing your websites there are issues that should be considered for each of these.

Search engines

If you are running an intranet and/or hosting your own website, you will probably have server software to manage the site. These usually contain some form of free search engine that can be used on your site. However, while these can do a decent job they are limited in terms of their power and functionality.

If you want to give your users the best search experience then you should look at buying a bespoke search engine. While these can be expensive, it will make a significant difference to the search experience of the users on your websites. Research the market thoroughly though to make sure you get the best product for your specific needs.

Metadata

As far as creating Web pages so that they can be found by search engines, one of the best options is to add metadata to pages. This can be thought of as information about information i.e. it is data that describes what is on the page. Most search engines use metadata to create the indexes which are used when looking for pages. Metadata is added to Web pages as metatags, which are included in the code of a page (usually in the Head section of an HTML document). There are a number of different elements that can be included in the metadata for a Web page including:

- Title

- Keywords

- Subject

- Description

- Publisher

- Date

Hot tip

Always get a demo from any companies from whom you are interested in buying a search engine. Also, if possible, ask if the demo can be done with your own data. This will make it more realistic and enable you to see results with content from your sites.

Don't forget

For a detailed look at searching on the Web, have a look at Get to No.1 on Google in the In Easy Steps series.

Adding metadata

Metadata is broken down into different categories, or elements, which describe a particular item of metadata. These have different methods of classification. One of the standard methods is the Dublin Core. This lists the various categories into which metadata can be grouped.

Some points to consider when adding metadata to websites:

- Ensure that the search engine on the website is capable of interpreting metadata. There is limited value in adding metadata to documents on the site if the search engine cannot be configured to search over these items. Check with the IT Administrator to ascertain the capabilities of your search engine. If it cannot utilize metadata it would be worthwhile finding a system that can, as the long-term benefits will outweigh any short-term costs

- Produce guidelines for adding metadata. This will cover areas such as who is responsible for adding metadata and how it is done e.g. through an automated system or manually

- Produce guidelines for inserting metadata retrospectively. This will be an issue for mature sites that have not had metadata added at the start of their lifetime. For consistency, metadata will be required for the whole site, not just new pages. Otherwise the search results will most likely be incomplete and therefore inaccurate

- Decide whether metadata will be applied centrally or by the authors of specific pages

- If metadata is added by individual authors of pages this will result in a large number of people adding metadata. If this is the case, ensure that they stick to the metadata guidelines to ensure consistency

- If possible, use a standard list for adding keywords. This is a list of words that are common to all areas of your organization and its use ensures consistency

- Create a list of keywords that are unique to your own organization (this could include legal terms, or phrases that are only used within your organization)

Don't forget

Dublin Core refers to Dublin in Ohio, where the standards were developed in the 1990s.

128

- Know your audience and make metatags concise, straightforward and meaningful

- Do not use any terms that could be ambiguous or offensive

- Remember that users all search for information in different ways. Try to accommodate several different options when adding metadata

- Perform test searches to see the results that are returned once metadata has been added to pages. Also, try 'before and after' searches to see the effect adding metadata has on search results for the same page

- Avoid using acronyms or special characters in metadata

The appearance of metadata

For HTML pages, such as those used on most websites, metadata is added to the HEAD part of the document, which is enclosed between the <head></head> tags in the document. In the source code the metadata will look similar to this:

<head>

<title>My Intranet Home Page</title>

<meta http-equiv="Content-Type" content="text/html; charset=iso-8859-1">

<meta name="description" content="This is the intranet homepage of My Business. Its aim is to provide you all with up to date, current and useful information about our business and what is happening. We have a mix of business and non-business information for all aspects of your time at work.">

<meta name="keywords" content="intranet, homepage, business, non-business, information, updates, news, social, notices">

<meta name="author" content="Nick Vandome, Intranet Team">

<meta name="date" content="15 October 2012">

<meta http-equiv="title" content="My Intranet Home Page">

</head>

Hot tip

To view the metadata on a website access the source code (View> Source or View>Source Code from your browser's menu bar).

129

Creating an Owner Network

If an intranet is designed, implemented and managed effectively then it should be viewed as a communications tool for everyone. There should be a sense of ownership so that all users feel it is something that is being done for their benefit and, as such, they feel a responsibility to ensure that the content is as accurate and up to date as possible.

Updating content

Keeping content up to date and fresh is essential to the evolution of an intranet: if content becomes stagnant then users will quickly turn away from it. Just as there is nothing appealing about drinking stagnant water, so no one wants to look at stagnant content and it is one way to guarantee that people will quickly turn away from the intranet

> Just as there is nothing appealing about drinking stagnant water, so no one wants to look at stagnant content

One way to ensure content is as up to date as possible is to create a network of content owners. These are people from sections throughout the organization who are responsible for updating the content for their area and also providing new content. Ideally there should be at least two content owners for each section, to cover for holidays or illness. If one content owner is not going to be available then they should inform their own manager, and the person who is going to cover, as well as the person who is responsible for managing the content owners.

Working with content owners

Once content owners have been identified, put all of their names in a spreadsheet, along with a schedule for how frequently they are to provide updates. Ideally this should be at least one a month, but they can also provide new content at any other time too. Each content owner should be contacted at the appropriate time and asked if they have any updates or amendments to their content. This can then be entered into the content owner spreadsheet as the 'last updated' date. Even if there are no changes this should still be noted as it indicates that the site owner has checked their content and confirmed that it is correct at that date.

Don't forget

Make sure that the role of content owner is a recognized task and that people are given the appropriate amount of time to do it effectively. It should not be something that is included in their duties as an afterthought.

Providing instructions

Site owners should be given instructions for what to look at in terms of content and some of these are:

- Checking dates. Anything that has a date on it is in danger of becoming redundant. For instance, if something says, 'We will give you a further update on 15 September' and someone is reading it in October and there has been no update, then questions could justifiably be asked. Always check dates and ensure that if an action has to be taken by a certain time then the necessary action is undertaken, whether it is to contact someone else for content, or update it yourself

- Checking updates. If you have been provided with information to put on your section of the intranet, it will become your responsibility to ensure that it is suitable and presented in an appropriate way

- Accuracy. Always check, and re-check, any facts and figures that are provided within content for your site. Even if you think something is correct, it is always worth checking it before it goes live

- Clarity. Does the content on your site make sense? You will be the first judge of this and if you feel it is not clear then you can ask the author to rewrite it, or you can edit it yourself. If you are unsure about the clarity of an article, ask someone else to read it to get a second opinion

- Appropriateness. Content should never be put on the intranet just for the sake of it, or to say that you have published new content. For any piece of content, ask yourself what purpose it serves and who is the intended audience

- Checking overall content. Although it is a recurring task, the overall content of each section should be checked each time a content owner is asked for an update

An initial meeting should be held with the content owners. One reason for this is to create a personal relationship with them, rather than just being someone at the end of an email. In addition, it is a good idea to have quarterly meetings too, just to deal with any issues that may occur and also to discuss any ideas for new content on the site.

Beware

The role of content owner is a very important one as they will be ultimately responsible for the content on their area of the intranet.

Catching People's Attention

Although intranets differ from websites in that you have more of a captive audience, you still need to catch people's attention to the point that they want to look at the intranet in the first instance. There are two main ways to do this:

- Update content as regularly as possible

- Include non-business items

Updating
If users know that they will being seeing new content each time that they view the intranet then it will give them more of an incentive to look at it to see what is happening.

Social items
There is some debate about this among communication professionals and web managers. Some think that social information is frivolous and detracts from the core business of the organization. However, although we may like to think the opposite, very few people work flat out every minute that they are at work. We all like to find out what we could have for lunch, see what is happening with any social clubs in the organization and see what our colleagues are up to in terms of charity work or sporting events.

The idea of publishing something like your canteen menu on the intranet can be a contentious one. However, this is frequently the most visited page on the site. Looking forward to lunch, or a coffee break, can be the highlight of the day and if people know what is available they can then get on with other tasks.

The important point to remember about social information is that it is not completely non-business related. If people open the intranet to look at the social information they may then stay to look at the business information too. Look at it as a loss-leader: sometimes you have to give away something for free to achieve success elsewhere. It will also give your intranet more credibility as the users will see that you are providing something just for them.

Keeping People's Attention

In some ways the easy part is to get people to visit your websites. Once you have got them there you have to ensure that they stay long enough so that you can get your messages across and then keep coming back.

The crucial thing to remember when people are viewing your websites is that, ultimately, it is all about the content. Although the design is important in terms of supporting what you have on the site, if people do not want to read what is on your site then you are fighting an uphill battle.

> If people do not want to read what is on your site then you are fighting an uphill battle

In addition to trying to make your written content as engaging as possible, there are a number ways in which you can try and encourage users to stay on your sites:

- Interaction. People always like to feel involved with things and if you give them this facility then they will be inclined to stay on the site longer ('stickability' as it is sometimes referred to). This can be in the form of online forums or discussion boards. Also, take a leaf out of the social media book and provide the means to comment on items or rate them. This not only gives everyone the chance to get involved on the site, it can also provide useful information about which pages and items are proving the most popular on the site

- Feedback. Everyone likes to have their views and opinions heard and one way to enable this is to provide means of feedback on your sites. Online surveys are an excellent way to gather feedback about a wide range of subjects and it enables the users to feel that they are involved in the decision-making process. However, if you conduct online surveys you will have to be prepared to act on the feedback that is given; it is not just a token gesture

- Content owners. Remember your content owners and work with them from a viewpoint of encouraging them to create the best content possible. If they are particularly interested in this you could source writing courses for them to attend

Beware

If you have forums or discussion boards, make sure that you have a robust policy regarding what can, and cannot, be posted with these tools. Also, give some thought as to whether they will be moderated or not.

Hot tip

Another feedback option is to provide quick surveys in the form of Yes/No questions. These can be done on a daily or weekly basis and include business and non-business items.

Accessibility Issues

When designing and managing websites one of the objectives should be to make the content available to as wide a range of users as possible, including those with disabilities such as blind or partially sighted users, or users with motor disabilities. The general term for this is accessibility.

Web Accessibility Initiative

Accessibility on the Web is a huge issue and there are literally hundreds of criteria over which accessibility can be checked. Thankfully, help is at hand through the Web Accessibility Initiative (WAI). This is an initiative run by the World Wide Web Consortium (W3C) which aims to provide best practice in Web standards, including accessibility.

The W3C website at www.w3.org has a wealth of information about its work and how to apply different Web standards. There is also a comprehensive section on accessibility at www. w3.org/WAI.

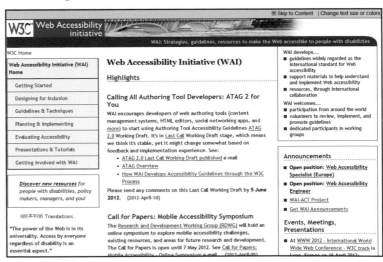

One of the main resources created by WAI is the Web Content Accessibility Guidelines (WCAG) 2.0. These are intended for Web authors and developers so that they can apply accessibility standards to their websites.

With the WCAG there are 12 guidelines and each one of these has levels of success ratings depending on how well a website meets each guideline. The ratings are A, AA and AAA.

Don't forget

A lot of websites have an accessibility link that explains their policy and approach to accessibility.

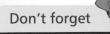
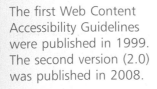

Don't forget

The first Web Content Accessibility Guidelines were published in 1999. The second version (2.0) was published in 2008.

Accessibility tools

There are a number of tools on the Web that will check your websites and provide a report about their level of accessibility. A lot of these work in a similar way: you enter the Web address (URL) of the website you want to check into the site's accessibility checker box and then you are sent a report of the accessibility issues on your site.

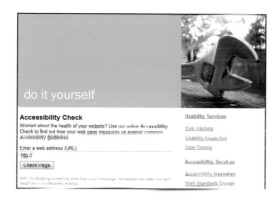

Some accessibility issues

The WCAG covers such a range of issues that it would be hard for every website to adhere fully to all of them. In a lot of instances it will be a case of trying to fulfill as many of the guidelines as possible. Some of the major areas for accessibility that can realistically be dealt with are:

- Using text alternatives for images. Images should always have a textual description added to them so that people using screen readers can hear a description of images

- Avoiding key information as text in graphics. Do not include instructions as part of a graphic

- Changing text size and background color. Have functionality so that users can change the size of text on a website and also the background color

- Text only alternative. Have an option so that users can view a site without any images at all

- Providing access through the keyboard. Some users with motor issues have difficulty using a mouse so all functionality should also be provided through keystrokes on the keyboard

135

Some Web Dos and Don'ts

When you are involved in the daily publishing for a website it can be easy to get caught up in the need to make content available as soon as possible. However, it is always a good idea to take a few moments to check that you are following some basic rules. Some Dos and Don'ts to try and follow are:

Dos

- Do make content a priority. Add, or update, content on a daily basis if possible

- Do think of your users. They are the lifeblood of your websites and your most important factor

- Do include non-business information on an intranet. Include things for the users and they will feel a greater sense of ownership for the site

- Do involve other people in the content creation process

- Do try and get all of your users involved in your sites, through feedback and surveys

- Do try new techniques and technologies. If something does not work, try something else

Don'ts

- Don't take things for granted once you have a website up and running. This is where the hard work really begins to keep it fresh and up to date

- Don't publish things just for the sake of it. Better to say nothing than publish padding or waffle

- Don't forget about your navigation. If users cannot get around easily they will leave your site

- Don't forget to cater for different age groups

- Don't forget about accessibility issues. Everyone should have access to your websites

- Don't take criticism personally. Everyone has a view about the look and feel of websites and you will always receive some adverse comments. However, listen to feedback and act upon it if necessary

Writing for the Web

This chapter shows how to produce clear and effective content specifically for websites, including formatting text and design issues.

How Web and Paper Differ

It may be stating the obvious, but reading from paper and a Web page on a computer monitor are very different experiences. It is accepted that it is harder, and more tiring, reading text from a screen. One of the main reasons for this is the glare from a computer screen, which is more tiring on the eyes, particularly over a sustained period of time:

- The majority of users always scan a Web page, particularly in the first instance. This is to get a quick sense of what is on the page. Remember, most pages have a lot more content than just text and the users will want to take all of this in as quickly as possible

- Less than 20% of users read word-by-word from a website (Jakob Nielsen). Some of this may be generational, with the younger generations tending to spend less time reading

- Reading from a monitor is about 25% slower than from paper. This has an impact on the length of articles, paragraphs and sentences

- Web pages should be approximately 50% smaller in terms of word count than the paper original

Writing for the screen

When creating content for websites it is important to remember that you are dealing with a different medium to paper documents. Some points about this to consider are:

- Think electronically. Always keep in mind that people will be reading your content from a screen rather than paper. If you fully understand the techniques for creating Web content then you should always try and apply them when applicable

Beware

Creating good written content for the Web can be a time-consuming task but it is worth ensuring you have the time and resource to do it properly.

- Do not just reproduce hard copy electronically. When creating documents for the Web it should not just be a case of copying and pasting the content from a hard copy document. Look at the text and see how it can be adapted for use on the Web, while still retaining the original message

Look at the text and see how it can be adapted for use on the Web, while still retaining the original message

- Create a visual roadmap. This is a technique for guiding the user through a Web page just by looking at it and scanning the content. (See the next two pages for more details about creating a roadmap)

- Dealing with long documents/manuals. Long documents, such as manuals, present a particular problem on the Web. The best way to deal with them is to break the content up into manageable sections and then format each section as you would for any other type of Web content. One important element is to ensure that there is sufficient navigation for the user to be able to find their way around the whole document. This may involve including main and secondary navigation as a self-contained function for the document. Also, ensure that there are enough hyperlinks within each section to enable the user to access related items

- Keep sentences short, concise and punchy. Check your own prose and also that of your contributors. This is even more important for Web writing than it is for hard copy

- Use one idea per paragraph, even if it is a single sentence. A lot of Web content consists of one sentence paragraphs. The BBC website is a good examples of this. (See page 142 for examples)

- Use short words rather than longer ones: remove all jargon where possible

- Print out Web pages and read them out loud to see if they still make sense

Don't forget

If you include links to move to other parts of a long document, make sure that there is a means for the user to get back to the original page too.

Creating a Roadmap

When users read Web pages they do so by scanning the page to find pieces of information that are meaningful or useful. Because of this it is important to create a visual roadmap that users can follow when they initially look at a Web page. This helps to guide them through the page and find the information that they need quickly. Some elements to consider when creating a visual roadmap:

- Start with the conclusion first, so users do not have to read the whole page if they do not want to

- Highlight key words and phrases - use bold or colored text for highlighting

---

Good Format

When users read Web pages they do so by **scanning** the page to find pieces of information that are meaningful or useful.

Because of this it is important to create a **visual roadmap** that users can follow when they initially look at a Web page.

- Use hyperlinks for additional information

Good Format

When users read Web pages they do so by **scanning** the page to find pieces of information that are meaningful or useful.

Because of this it is important to create a **visual roadmap** that users can follow when they initially look at a Web page.

Additional links:

See examples of poor format

Read more about visual roadmaps

Beware

Humor can be very subjective so it is best leaving it out of business websites, rather than running the risk of upsetting people.

- Avoid hyperlinks containing 'Web terms' e.g. 'Click Here', or 'Follow this link'. Use hyperlinks that contain meaningful information

- Use meaningful headings - avoid humor or puns

- Use bulleted and numbered lists

Elements of a roadmap

This helps to guide them through the page and find the information that they need quickly. Elements of a roadmap can be presented in a bulleted list:

- Start with the conclusion first, so users don't have to read the whole page if they don't want to
- Highlight key words and phrases — use **bold** or **colored text** for highlighting

Or a numbered list:

1. Use sidebars for additional information
2. Use hyperlinks for navigation
3. Use a breadcrumb trail to let users know where they are

- Use pull quotes to break up text (see page 143). These are quotes that are taken from the text and enlarged so that they stand out from the rest of the normal sized text

- Use sidebars for additional information that enhances the main article but is not a crucial part of it (see page 143)

- Use images to break up text and introduce a graphical element into the Web page. However, make sure that any images are relevant to the text, give them clear captions that are not too large - they should enhance the text, not overshadow it

- Use CSS formatting (stylesheets) to create layouts that can look more like desktop publishing

- Use 'Next Page' and 'Previous Page' links. This can be used to break up documents, but always make sure that the links go to the correct pages

- Create a breadcrumb trail at the top of each page, as described in Chapter Seven

Don't forget

Images should always have a textual 'Alt' tags attached to them in the code of the page. This is to enable blind or partially-sighted users to use a Web reader to hear the text alternative for images. Make sure that the Alt tag is as meaningful a description of the image as possible.

Paragraph Length

Because it is harder to read text on screen than it is on paper, any methods of making text more readable are usually more pronounced on websites. One area in which this is the case is paragraph length.

For hard copy documents it is best to keep paragraphs reasonably short. But because people are used to reading in this way paragraphs can still be up to approximately 5–10 sentences in length (as long as the sentences are reasonably short) and still contribute to a readable document.

However, on websites paragraphs should be much shorter, to give the users time to take in the information and to create a more appealing appearance so that they do not feel that they will be swamped with large blocks of text to read.

It is not unreasonable to use one sentence per paragraph on websites, as long as there is one idea in each sentence. At first, users may find this slightly unusual, but they will quickly get used to it and come to prefer the clear layout.

Using one sentence per paragraph can have a dramatic effect on your overall Web page layout.

Beware

Just because you try to limit the length of paragraphs, this does not mean that you have to dumb-down your writing. Short and concise can still be engaging and interesting.

142

For hard copy documents it is best to keep paragraphs reasonably short. But because people are used to reading in this way paragraph can still be up to approximately five sentences in length (as long as the sentences are reasonably short) and still contribute to a readable document. However, on websites paragraphs should be much shorter, to give the users time to take in the information and to create a more appealing appearance so that they do not feel that they will be swamped with large blocks of text to read. It is not unreasonable to use one sentence per paragraph on websites, as long as there is one idea in each sentence. At first unusual, but they will quickly the clear layout. Using one se dramatic effect on your overall

For hard copy documents it is best to keep paragraphs reasonably short.

But because people are used to reading in this way paragraph can still be up to approximately five sentences in length (as long as the sentences are reasonably short) and still contribute to a readable document.

However, on websites paragraphs should be much shorter, to give the users time to take in the information and to create a more appealing appearance so that they do not feel that they will be swamped with large blocks of text to read.

It is not unreasonable to use one sentence per paragraph on websites, as long as there is one idea in each sentence.

At first, users may find this slightly unusual, but they will quickly get used to it and come to prefer the clear layout.

Using one sentence per paragraph can have a dramatic effect on your overall Web page layout.

Breaking Up Text

As shown in Chapter Six there are a number of techniques that can be used to break up text on a page and make it easier to read. On websites there are two other items that can be used to highlight specific items and provide additional information to the main piece of content. These are:

- Sidebars

- Pull quotes

Sidebars

These are blocks of information that are provided as supplementary items to the main article. For instance, they may provide background information about an item that is mentioned in the main content. Sidebars are frequently used on colored background so that they not only standout but also help bring some variety to the design of the page.

Don't forget

Sidebars and pull quotes can both be used very effectively with hard copy publications too. However, they are particularly useful on websites in terms of breaking up text and adding to the overall roadmap on the page.

Pull quotes

This is a device where a piece of text (usually no longer than one sentence) is enlarged for emphasis. The pull quote can also be displayed in a different color, for added effect.

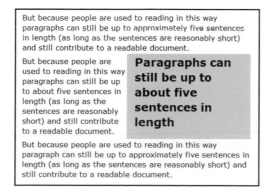

Formatting With Stylesheets

In the early days of Web design the majority of pages were created with HTML code. This specified the content and formatting within the same document. However, this could be cumbersome in that each time there was a change in formatting this would have to be included in the HTML document. For instance, each time a different font was used, this had to be specified in terms of font family, size and color.

In recent years cascading style sheets (CSS) have become more standard for designing Web pages. This is because they can be used to separate the content and presentation of Web pages. The content is still in the HTML document but the presentation (or formatting) is included within the CSS document in the form of a group of formatting rules. These can then be applied to multiple files. This means that if one of the rules is updated the appearance of the relevant content in all of the linked files is also updated, without the need to edit the individual HTML files. CSS rules can be used for formatting and positioning items.

CSS styles can be included directly in an HTML document, in which case they are usually located in the <head> section of the document, or they can be created in specific CSS files. These have a .css extension and can be linked to the HTML document. This is now a more common way of creating stylesheet documents: one stylesheet can be created and linked to all of the files within a site.

Linked stylesheets have the link contained in the <head> section of an HTML page:

Don't forget

Web pages now frequently have stylesheets for mobile devices as well as for standard Web display. When viewing on a mobile device, the browser will identify the correct stylesheet and so render the pages correctly for that device.

```
<head>
<meta http-equiv="Content-Type" content="text/html; charset=utf-8" />
<title>Untitled Document</title>
<link href="thrColLiqHdr.css" rel="stylesheet" type="text/css" /><!--[if lte IE 7]>
<style>
.content { margin-right: -1px; } /* this 1px negative margin can be placed on any of
the columns in this layout with the same corrective effect. */
ul.nav a { zoom: 1; }  /* the zoom property gives IE the hasLayout trigger it needs to
correct extra whiltespace between the links */
</style>
<![endif]-->
<link href="CSS/colors1.css" rel="stylesheet" type="text/css" />
</head>
```

Consistent and accessible

Stylesheets are a great way to ensure consistency across a website and they are also better from an accessibility point of view as the HTML file does not have to contain a lot of complicated formatting as this is all done via the CSS file.

Appearance of CSS

CSS files can be complex in their construction as they frequently contain formatting for an entire site. Because of this it is usually Web authors and developers who are responsible for creating the CSS files. In some cases they will be given a design and then asked to create a CSS file to replicate this for the website. The code for a CSS file looks like this:

```
body {
    font: 100%/1.4 Verdana, Arial, Helvetica, sans-serif;
    background: #4E415C;
    margin: 0;
    padding: 0;
    color: #000;
}

/* ~~ Element/tag selectors ~~ */
ul, ol, dl { /* Due to variations between browsers, it's
    padding: 0;
    margin: 0;
}
h1, h2, h3, h4, h5, h6, p {
    margin-top: 0;   /* removing the top margin gets aroul
    padding-right: 15px;
    padding-left: 15px; /* adding the padding to the side
}
a img { /* this selector removes the default blue border
    border: none;
}
```

Some web authoring programs (such as Dreamweaver from Adobe) have extensive tools for creating CSS and also templates that are already created with elements of CSS.

145

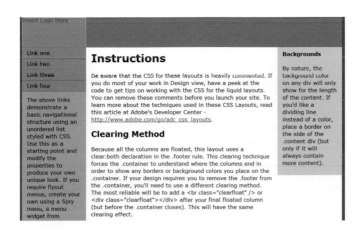

Insert Logo Here

Link one
Link two
Link three
Link four

The above links demonstrate a basic navigational structure using an unordered list styled with CSS. Use this as a starting point and modify the properties to produce your own unique look. If you require flyout menus, create your own using a Spry menu, a menu widget from

Instructions

Be aware that the CSS for these layouts is heavily commented. If you do most of your work in Design view, have a peek at the code to get tips on working with the CSS for the liquid layouts. You can remove these comments before you launch your site. To learn more about the techniques used in these CSS Layouts, read this article at Adobe's Developer Center - http://www.adobe.com/go/adc_css_layouts.

Clearing Method

Because all the columns are floated, this layout uses a clear:both declaration in the .footer rule. This clearing technique forces the .container to understand where the columns end in order to show any borders or background colors you place on the .container. If your design requires you to remove the .footer from the .container, you'll need to use a different clearing method. The most reliable will be to add a <br class="clearfloat" /> or <div class="clearfloat"></div> after your final floated column (but before the .container closes). This will have the same clearing effect.

Backgrounds

By nature, the background color on any div will only show for the length of the content. If you'd like a dividing line instead of a color, place a border on the side of the .content div (but only if it will always contain more content).

Using Graphical Elements

We all like looking at pictures and on websites they can be a significant advantage in creating a roadmap: images give the users a quick indication of what is being dealt with on a specific page.

However, when using images on websites there are some issues that should be addressed:

- Do not use images just for the sake of it. There should be a purpose for every graphical element on a website, rather than adding them because you think you should

- Add captions if necessary. This will help the users put the images into context and it is another useful roadmap item

146

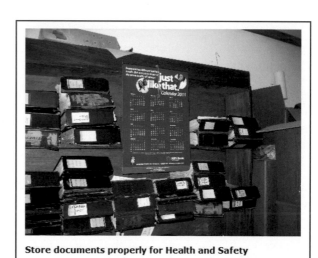

Store documents properly for Health and Safety

- Make sure that images are optimized for use on the Web. This means that the file size is not too large, so they will download more quickly on the site. Image editing programs such as Photoshop are ideal for reducing the file size of images for the Web

- Do not make images appear too large on a Web page. They should complement the content that is already there, rather than overshadow it

- Always add ALT tags for accessibility

- Graphical elements can be used in navigation bars as well as within the main body of a page

Is Content Management the Answer?

Content Management Systems (CMS) have, at times, been promoted as the answer to a range of communications issues. This chapter looks at the facts and myths about using a CMS. It assesses when to use a CMS and shows how to implement and manage one.

CMS Overview

Before we look at the workings and benefits of a Content Management System (CMS) it is worth stating what it is not. It is not a silver bullet that will solve all of the communication issues (and everything else) in your organization. Although this may seem obvious, this is sometimes how they are portrayed by the companies trying to sell them.

It is just software

When considering a CMS it is necessary to look at a variety of different products, which inevitably involves attending demonstration sessions covering what they can do. These are obviously geared to making the product look as good as possible and by the end of it you may feel that they can do everything, including bringing you your coffee first thing in the morning. These demonstrations are designed to look very slick and show how easy it is to create, collate, approve, find and publish information. It is true that this is the function of a CMS but what you should keep at the forefront of your mind is that it is a software system at the end of the day (albeit a very powerful one in a lot of cases) and it has to be properly installed, rolled-out and implemented to get the maximum benefit from it.

Do you need a CMS?

Using a CMS is not generally an inexpensive option and before your organization goes down this route you should think carefully as to whether you really need a CMS. After the bright lights and slick presentation of the sales pitch, sit down with key people, from all areas of your organization and assess the pros and cons of using a CMS. Some areas to consider are:

- Does everyone understand the reasons for using a CMS?

- Does everyone understand the workings of a CMS? Everyone involved should know what a CMS does, and what it does not do too

- Which areas in the organization will use the CMS and for what purposes?

- Who will manage the IT side of the CMS: will it be in-house or an external company?

- Who will have overall responsibility of content on the CMS? This should usually be the communications section

Beware

A CMS in itself is not the answer to any communication problems that you have in your organization. It has to be implemented and managed properly to give you the foundation to start improving your communications.

Defining a CMS

So what is a CMS?

Essentially a CMS is a system that should make it easier for an organization to create, publish and control content, throughout the business. This is usually done via websites, but there are also other options. It is important to remember that a CMS itself is not a website: it can be used to create and manage these but it is essentially a system for managing information.

Some of the functions of a CMS include:

- Creating content with easy to use templates. The content authors usually fill in text fields within the templates and when this is published it populates the design template for the website

- Creating template designs. These remain fixed and cannot be edited unless by an administrator. This means that the content authors do not have to worry about design when they are creating their content. Also, the administrators do not have to worry about anyone changing the consistency of design of the site, either accidentally, or on purpose

- Allowing multiple users to create and publish content. Dozens, or hundreds, of different people can enter content into a CMS but this is something that should be planned and managed carefully

- Creating a workflow of create, approve, publish. This enables people at different levels to create content and more senior ones to approve it, if required

- Creating a publishing schedule. This can include setting dates for items to be published and removed automatically

- Creating tagged content for searching purposes

- Providing a powerful search facility. A CMS frequently has a search facility built-in to it and this can be one of the key selling points of a system

- Harnessing databases. This is another key feature of a CMS. If you work with a lot of large databases, a CMS can be used to manage the data and present it to the end user. Sites such as Amazon are a good example of large databases managed by a CMS

Don't forget

A CMS separates out the content and the design of a website. The CMS is responsible for the content and this then feeds into a separate design. This enables people to create content on the CMS without having to worry about web design as it is already in place.

Assessing a CMS

What do you want it for?

The first thing that you should do before you start considering a CMS is to work out exactly what you want it for. You should specify your full requirements in terms of functionality, rather than buying a system and then trying to work out how to best use it. The software should fit your needs rather than trying to shoe-horn what you want to do into a CMS that is not suitable for you.

One important point to remember is that a CMS should not be bought just because it is thought to be the latest must-have business accessory. It has to be an informed decision, based on the needs of the business and the benefit which a CMS can bring. In this respect, the best people to assess the system are those who will be using it for communications purposes. Although the final decision may lie with the CEO or director of finance, this should be reached after consultation and advice from the communications experts.

> The software should fit your needs rather than trying to shoe-horn what you want into a CMS that is not suitable for you

150

Considering a business case

Since a CMS is a significant investment it will probably require a business case to justify the cost and demonstrate the benefits which it will bring. This will include the requirements from the system for your business.

Assessing your requirements

When assessing your requirements in terms of a CMS there are several areas to consider:

● How powerful will the system need to be i.e. how many servers will you require to host and run the CMS? You will need to consult with you IT experts about this and also other areas of the business, to see how they want to use the CMS

● Migration of existing content. Will the CMS be required to migrate existing content e.g. from your intranet or Internet site, or will all content be created from scratch?

- Design. You do not have to use a CMS for the design of websites, but you can do. This involves creating templates into which the completed content items are published. The design of these templates will have to be specified so that they can be created within the CMS

- Workflow. The way in which you want content to be created and published also has to be specified. The most common workflow is Author, Reviewer and Publisher. However, workflows can be considerably more complicated than this so you will need to work out who is going to create the content and the subsequent stages that it needs to go through before it is published

- Content types. Within a CMS there are usually different content types, which determine the appearance of content when it is published. For instance, you may want a News item and a Vacancy item to have a different look and feel and so this will require two separate content types. A content type is essentially a template for a specific category of content. The elements of each content type have to be specified clearly in terms of items such as font type and size, headings, images and mandatory fields (see below)

- Each content item will have different mandatory fields that require to be populated before a new piece of content can be published on the system

- Databases. If the CMS is going to be using information from databases, the types of databases have to be specified, as does the method by which this will be transferred to the CMS. Since this can be a highly technical issue, it has to be specified, with close liaison with your IT department

Types of CMS

There are a large number of CMSs on the market, of varying type and power. The main types that are available are:

- Bespoke. These are CMSs that are designed and built by the supplier of the system i.e. it is their own system that they have created. This is done with their own bespoke code which can usually only be changed by the supplier, or an agent working on their behalf. The advantage of this type of system is that they are powerful and can be fully supported by the supplier as they know the system in-depth

- Online. These are CMSs that can be downloaded from the Web and then customized for your own use. The author part of the CMS is downloaded to your own computer and once the content has been created it has to be hosted by a company specializing in this (although you should be able to do it on your own internal servers too). Two of these types of CMSs are provided by Joomla (www.joomla.com) and Wordpress (http://wordpress.org). These types of CMSs are generally straightforward to use and you can get up and running with them quickly

Don't forget

Online CMSs such as Joomla and Wordpress are open source systems. These are created, and enhanced, by hundreds of programmers, who usually work on the software for free and for the love of it.

- Open source. These are CMSs that are created with open source code. This is where the source code is made available for anyone to work on and improve, rather than locked code that is provided with a bespoke system. It is frequently created within public forums and because of its collaborative nature it tends to be cheaper and also is of a high quality

Creating a CMS Project Team

Over 60% of CMS projects fail (BT) so it is essential that a project team is put in place to manage the whole project. This should cover the initial assessment of a CMS through to the final implementation and delivery. The project team, or elements of it, could also remain in place once the system has been delivered, to work on developments and improvements.

Depending on your organization's method of project management, there will be a process that will need to be followed in order to start the CMS project. This should be along the lines of:

- Creating a Project Initiation Document (PID)
- Creating a Business Case
- Creating a Project Team

Creating a PID
A PID is used to define the project, to form the basis for its management and assessment of overall success. It covers:

- What the project is aiming to achieve
- Why it is important to achieve it
- Where it will be developed
- Who is going to be involved in managing it and their responsibilities
- How and when it is going to happen

Creating a Business Case
A CMS is a considerable commitment in terms of both cost and resource, so a full business case should be created to justify its use. This should include:

- The reasons for using a CMS
- The uses to which it will be put
- Costs
- Benefits
- Risk Log

Don't forget

The Project Team should meet at least once a month during the duration of the CMS project, to keep up to date with progress and make any decisions that are required.

Makeup of a Project Team

The makeup of the Project Team will vary depending on the size of the organization and the proposed reach of the CMS but some of the roles included should be:

- Senior Responsible Officer (SRO). This is the person who has overall responsibility for the project. They do not necessarily have to be an expert in the subject but they should have a good working knowledge of the project. Although they will not be directly involved in all aspects of the project, they will ultimately be answerable to the Executive Board

- Project Manager. This is the person who is responsible for the day to day running of the project. They will have to liaise with everyone involved with the project and also create the documents such as the Business Case and other similar items

- Communications representatives. Although a CMS, as such, is not necessarily a communications device, the items that it drives, i.e. websites, most definitely are. Therefore communications should be at the heart of the Project Team and have the most input into the end product that is going to be created with the CMS

- IT representatives. A CMS is a complex and powerful piece of software so it is important that members of your organization's IT department are involved so that can help with the installation and also assess the impact it may have on other systems

- Installation representatives. There should also be representatives from the people who are undertaking the installation. This may be from the company that is providing the CMS, or a third party

Specification Documents

In addition to the Business Case there should be two other documents, the Creative Specifications and the Technical Specifications. These are the documents from which the supplier will work to install the CMS and create the design and functionality of any websites powered by the CMS. Two important points to remember about these documents:

- Write everything down, do not presume anything. The specification documents will be used to build your system so you should narrate everything in as much detail as possible. If you want titles on your Web pages to appear in a certain shade of blue, note down the exact requirements. For this reason, specifications are usually very long, complex documents

> You should narrate everything in as much detail as possible

- If a change has to be made as a result of something that has been omitted from the specification documents, you may be charged for it and it could also cause a delay to the project

The Creative Specification

This document lays out the look and feel of any websites that will be powered by the CMS. It also details the functionality in terms of elements of the site. For instance, if you want to enable users to customize certain parts of the site, this should be included in the Creative Spec in terms of what they can do and how it will look. Elements of the Creative Spec can include the design of the site and also any additional elements that are introduced.

The Technical Specification

This document is aimed at the IT side of the CMS. It covers the installation of the CMS and how it will be used in relation to your computer systems. Therefore this is an area for IT experts, who should work closely with the supplier who is installing the CMS system.

It is essential that the Technical Spec is checked as thoroughly as possible: mistakes made at this stage could prove to be very costly if they cause major changes during the installation process.

Installing a CMS

A CMS is a complex piece of software and installing it is not for the faint-hearted. It will require to be installed on existing servers within your organization, or new ones will have to be put in place for installation. This is work that should be undertaken by your IT department and/or the company who is providing the CMS. Because of this, it is important that your IT experts are included in the process of assessing a CMS from the beginning.

Although a lot of the technical side of setting up the CMS will be done by the IT experts there are some areas that you should be aware of. In some cases you will be involved in developing or working on them:

Don't forget

Because of the different versions of the CMS that need to be set up (for previewing, testing and backup) you may need several servers to host the entire system.

- Backup for the main system. Due to the amount of information that can be stored on a CMS it is essential that everything on it is backed up, at least on a daily basis. Before the system is commissioned, the backup should be fully tested to ensure that any lost content can be restored

> Before the system is commissioned the backup should be fully tested

- Preview site. This is an area where authors can preview their work, to view it as it will appear, before it is published

- Test site. In addition to the full site there should also be a test site. This is used for installing patches and software updates to ensure that they work before they are rolled-out to the live site. The test site is different from the preview site

- Load testing. Depending on the size of the organization there could be hundreds, or thousands, of concurrent users accessing information from the CMS at any one time. Therefore the system has to be tested to ensure that it can cope with these levels of use

- Impact on other systems. It is important to assess how the CMS may affect all of the other IT systems

- Security. This covers security from viruses and malware and covers internal systems to which the CMS is connected and also any public facing ones

Rolling Out a CMS

In some respects, using a CMS can be a major communications change for an organization, but in others the end user may not notice huge differences. Since the CMS will most likely be used to power internal and external websites, the majority of people may not necessarily be aware of its existence. However, having said that, there will hopefully be a range of features that will make the Web experience better for everyone involved.

Promoting the CMS

Regardless of the physical impact the CMS may have on the people within an organization it is still important that they know about it. They should be told:

- Why it is being used

- The expected benefits

- The functions performed by the CMS

- The changes that people will see in terms of new features on the intranet or external website

How people are told these things will depend on the size of an organization but there are various options:

- One of the most effective ways is to hold seminars to demonstrate what the CMS does. This gives people the chance to see the system in operation and ask questions

- A training video about the system can also be produced

- Details can also be published on the intranet, either as static form or, again, using video

Roles and Responsibilities

One of the great things about a CMS is that it expands the Web publishing process to, potentially, anyone in an organization. However, with this flexibility comes a responsibility to make sure that the right people are given the correct roles and that everyone is aware of their responsibilities within the CMS.

Identifying the authors

One of the most important tasks to undertake before a CMS is introduced as a live system is to identify content authors in different areas of the organization. These will be the people who will be responsible for creating and adding content on the CMS.

When identifying content authors, the following should be considered in relation to the role:

- Are the prospective authors good writers? Regardless of their position in the organization, content authors have to be able to create accurate, interesting and engaging content. Some aspects of this can be learnt, but good writing is something instinctive that some people have and others do not. Also, content authors should enjoy writing as this may be something that becomes a bigger part of their job

- Do content authors have enough time for the role, or can time be made for them? Authoring content on the CMS should not be something that is done as an afterthought once everything else is completed. Once someone has been identified as a content author, it should be recognized as part of their job description and the necessary time allocated to it

- What level of authority do content authors have? Although this may seem irrelevant in terms of putting content onto the CMS it is important as they will need to have the assertiveness to tell people if their content is not appropriate or suitable. In this respect it does not matter too much what level they inhabit within the organization; in terms of the CMS they should be viewed as experts and their opinions should be accepted as such

Beware

Content authors should not be forced into the role if they do not want to do it. Authors should be enthusiastic about doing the role, otherwise it could impact on the quality of the content on the CMS.

Assigning reviewers

In many respects, the role of the reviewer is the most important one in the CMS workflow. This is the role that is responsible for checking a piece of content and then approving it for publication. Although some roles can be shared by a single person on the CMS, the author and reviewer should usually be different people. This is because it can be harder to check your own work and also because the role of reviewer has more responsibility so the person doing this may not have time to do the authoring too. Also, it is good practice to assign different people to different parts of the workflow, so that if one person is not available it only affects one part of the workflow, not all of it.

> In many respects, the role of the reviewer is the most important one in the CMS workflow

The reviewer is the person who checks a piece of content and approves it for publication. Therefore it should be people in the organization who can take responsibility if there is a mistake in a piece of content or an issue with it after it is published.

Using publishers

The publisher is the person who puts the finished pieces of content onto the live CMS. They will require to have some technical knowledge of the system and also be available to publish content whenever it has been approved. Usually, there is a system whereby the publisher is notified when a new piece of content is ready for publication. This is done either by email or within their own area of the CMS console. The role of publisher can also be combined with those of either author and reviewer.

Arranging cover

There may be a number of people within an organization assigned to each role on the CMS. This ensures that a backlog of work does not build up and that one person is not swamped by work in their role. Also, it is important to have people trained so that they can provide cover for people when they are on holiday or off sick. They should be given the opportunity to work on the live system rather than just wait until someone is unavailable.

Don't forget

Although they do not need to work together, reviewers and authors should know each other so that they can discuss any issues or problems that arise.

Keeping Control

One of the fundamental principles of a CMS is that it potentially allows anyone within an organization to create and publish content. This can be a great advantage, but it can also be a disadvantage, in terms of keeping control.

Know your authors

Overall control for content on the CMS should lie within the Communications section. This may seem a bit prescriptive, but if there is no central control over what goes onto the CMS then

the standard of content will decline quickly. This cannot only be frustrating for all involved, but it can affect the integrity of what is published via the CMS. Once people start to question the quality of information that is produced then they will be less likely to consume the content. Perhaps more importantly, they may start to be less trustful about what they are told.

Keeping control of what could be potential publishing anarchy is one of the challenges of managing a CMS. In order to ensure control over the content the first thing to do is to have a list of all of your content authors, including their contact details. The reasons for this are:

> ## Keeping control is one of the challenges of managing a CMS

- So you know who is responsible for content for different areas and can contact them if required. Usually, authors will be responsible for creating content within their area e.g. content for the finance section will be created by finance authors

- So you know who to contact for any training that is required on the CMS or training covering content creation issues. Training for the CMS, and the content on it, should be ongoing and there should be a regular schedule for refreshing training and updating authors' awareness of what is expected of them and the standard of content they are supposed to create on the system

Training your authors

Content authors should receive training before they start working on the CMS. This should cover:

- The workings of the system. This does not have to be to the level of an IT developer, but it should be enough so that the content authors are confident about using the CMS and have a good understanding of the elements used for content creation. This part of the training can be done by someone within your own organization with a good understanding of the CMS, or a trainer from the CMS supplier. Most companies have people who perform this service, for users of different levels of expertise

- Corporate guidelines for creating content. If you have corporate guidelines for publishing communications, this should be included in the CMS training. If you do not have this document, you should create one

- Good writing techniques. This could be a separate course but all content authors should be encouraged to think like writers, rather than someone who is just filling in a few text boxes on the CMS

- Writing for the Web. Chapter Eight looks at these issues and all content authors should be made fully aware of them so that they can create their content with this in mind

Relevant training should also be given to reviewers and publishers, although they may not need to know as much information about content creation.

Monitoring content

Think of monitoring content created from the CMS not as a policing role, but as a quality one. Even when items have been approved and published, keep looking over the site to ensure that content is accurate, up to date, engaging and presented in an appealing way. If you identify any issues this could be something that could be covered with training.

Don't forget

Writing for the Web should be seen as the same regardless of whether the site is created by a CMS or not.

Using the Power of a CMS

A CMS is an incredibly powerful piece of software and it would be under-used if it is just deployed to publish a static HTML website. The uses to which the CMS is to be put should be identified and agreed before the system is bought. But once it is in place there should be a definite effort made to make sure that the full power of the CMS is used. This is usually best done with collaboration between Communications and IT: Communications say what they would like to do and IT say whether it is possible and how it is going to be achieved.

Some uses to which a CMS can be put are:

- Automated publishing. This is when the times and dates can be specified for pieces of content to be published. The system then does this as the allotted time

- Blogs. A CMS is an effective vehicle for publishing and updating blogs. It can be used in the same way as a social media site, where other users can comment and rate an item. This creates a collaborative environment and makes users feel that they have a say in what happens on the system

- Forums. Interactive forums can also be managed with a CMS. These will probably require some form of moderation in terms of acceptable content, but it is another way in which interaction can be created with the CMS

- eCommerce. Since a CMS can harness the power of databases, they are excellent for managing eCommerce sites. They can be used to collate information from customers and also handle financial transactions and send out invoices

  ## CMS are excellent for managing eCommerce sites

- eMarketing. In terms of distributing information to a large audience for marketing purposes, a CMS is an excellent option as it can use a database of customer emails and then send out marketing information as required. It can also be used to monitor this in terms of how many emails have been opened and how many responses have been received for a specific campaign

10 Moving Pictures are Here

Video is starting to become a staple of corporate communications and this chapter shows how to use it in your organization.

Why Video Matters

The use of video on websites is probably the biggest development in communications on the Web in the last five years. It is now not uncommon to see video clips on external websites and also being used on intranets. Some of the ways that video is now being used for corporate communications are:

- News items

- Special events

- Social items

- Training

164

The great benefit about video is that it is consumed instantly, without too much effort by the recipient. It is also a good way to communicate with the younger generation of workers, who will have been brought up with videos on TV and the Web. As well as publishing video on the Web, more and more organizations are now installing television screens. These can be used for broadcasting network television programs, but there are also systems for playing your own video content too.

The great benefit about video is that it is consumed instantly

Some issues to remember about video though:

- For use on the Web, ensure, as far as possible, that all users have the means to view video. This is usually in the form of a video card and a media player such as Windows Media Player

- If the video contains a core message, ensure that this is also communicated in another format too. This will usually be in the form of a transcript on the intranet

- Train people properly for filming and editing video. It will quickly be obvious to the users if it is has been done in an amateurish fashion

- Do not feel you have to use video for everything. Be selective so that it has more impact when it is used. Better to create a small number of professional videos than dozens of poor ones

Capturing Video

Chapter Two details some of the equipment that is required to capture video content. A quick summary of this is:

- Cameras. Either professional standard or consumer video cameras would still do a reasonable job

- Tripods. Good quality tripods are essential to keep the cameras steady and get a clear shot

- Studio. Have some form of space that can be 'dressed' as a studio setting, using backgrounds and green screen

- Lighting. Even with the best cameras and studio, professional lighting can make all the difference

Filming techniques

Whoever is involved in filming video should be given appropriate training, which would usually be done by an external video training supplier. Also, these are some areas that should be considered when capturing video:

- Have one person in charge as the director

- Give people plenty of warning if you are going to be filming them, so that they can prepare themselves

- Have rehearsals so that people can feel as relaxed as possible

- If people are using autocue let them practice with it first

- Ask people to speak a bit slower than they normally do

- When filming, use a tripod whenever possible

- When zooming and panning, do so in a slow but steady fashion. Try and avoid jerky movements

Don't forget

Not many organizations have the luxury of having a full-time video team. Therefore it may be the case of training people who already have some of these skills and including it as part of their role.

165

Editing Video

There are a number of different video editing programs available, each offering different levels of power and functionality. They can differ significantly and can be broken down into two main categories:

- Professional programs

- Consumer programs

For all types of programs though the editing process is similar:

- Download the video into the editing program

- Create clips from the video

- Place the clips on the video timeline

- Add transitions between the clips

- Add additional elements such as titles, graphics and voiceovers

- Output the completed video into the required format e.g. as a file for the Web or a DVD

Professional programs

The industry standard video editing progam is Final Cut Pro which is used on the Apple Mac platform. The PC alternative is Adobe Premiere Pro. Both of these programs are very powerful but there is a significant learning curve and it is not something that you can pick up in a couple of weeks. A proper schedule of training should be undertaken for either of these programs, including hands-on training working with the software.

Beware

You do not have to add too many additional elements to video to make it effective. Do not go overboard with dramatic transitions and special effects.

Consumer programs

You do not need an expensive, state of the art, professional video editing program to produce perfectly acceptable video content, particularly if it is going to be broadcast over the Web. There are a lot of highly effective programs that can be used to edit and output video for a business environment. Three to look at are:

- VideoPad Editor. An excellent video editing program: reasonably priced with a wide range of functionality and reasonably easy to learn quickly

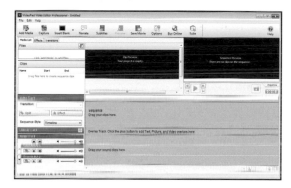

Don't forget

When editing video, use the most powerful computer possible as this will speed up the process. Traditionally, video editing professionals have tended to use Apple Mac computers for this.

167

- Premiere Elements. This is the consumer version of Premiere Pro from Adobe. It is a user-friendly option that also integrates closely with the photo editing program Elements

- iMovie. Another option for the Mac, this is the cheapest of the three consumer programs here and can be downloaded from the Apple App Store. It is very easy to use but does not have as much functionality as the other programs

Creating a Video Network

One of the most common ways of using video in the workplace is via computer desktops. This has the advantage that people can watch video when it suits them and they can select the items that most interest them. However, one of the disadvantages is that there is no way of checking if people have seen a particular item of video.

As well as broadcasting video on desktops, another option is to install a TV/Video network. This is a network of TV screens throughout the organization that can play video and TV content. This is becoming increasingly common in the workplace and is a good way to get messages across. There are a number of advantages to creating a video network:

- Different items can be scheduled to individual screens

- People do not have to watch all of an item at one time. They may see different parts of it at different times

- Static information can also be used on a network of this type, such as slides for one-off important messages

Communicating the change

Bringing a video network into an organization is an important strategic decision and so has to be communicated clearly to the workforce. Not only is it a significant investment, it will also be a cultural change for the organization. It should not just be imposed on people without any prior knowledge; if this is done then it may be met with negativity and animosity.

Hot tip

When introducing a video network, consult with the users first to see what they expect from this type of communications channel and what they would like to see on it. This should establish their buy-in and ensure that the network is well received.

When introducing a video network the communications strategy for it should cover the following:

- The objectives of the network. This should cover specific items rather than just saying that it will improve communications in the organization

- The benefits from the network

- The types of content that will be included

- Requests for people who are interested in contributing to the video network

How a network works

There are companies who specialize in creating and managing video networks. They should be able to provide all of the hardware and software, install the system and also provide training and support for whoever is working with the administration of it.

A video network of this kind works in the following way:

- The video content is uploaded to the servers of the company providing the system. It can also be uploaded onto the servers within your own organization

- Video is uploaded via an online console that can only be accessed by those people in the organization who are authorized to do so

- Once video has been uploaded it can then be scheduled to appear on the screen network. This can be done on a loop i.e. several pieces of content play one after another in a continuous loop until instructed to stop, or they can be scheduled to play at specific times

- Additional content types can also be scheduled, such as Powerpoint presentations, photographs and TV channels

- Depending on the type of system, each screen can be split and scheduled to display different items of content at the same time. For instance, the main area of the screen may be playing a news video from the organization, while along the bottom of the screen is a textual news ticker containing the latest sports, travel or weather news

Don't forget

When looking for a supplier for a video network system, make sure that ongoing support is included in the price. This should usually be on an annual basis and include service level agreements for how quickly issues on the system will be addressed.

Publishing Video on YouTube

One the great successes in the social media world is the video sharing website YouTube. This was launched in 2005 and has become the number one video sharing site on the Web. In 2006 it was taken over by Google but still retains its own identity.

Initially YouTube was designed to share personal video content, which covered just about everything imaginable. Since its early days though YouTube has become much more sophisticated and it is now also an important option for business organizations to publish video.

Using video on YouTube should be done as part of an integrated communications strategy, rather than a standalone product. Videos should be used to support other channels of communication and provide added value.

Hot tip

Include a link to your YouTube channel on your corporate website.

Creating an account

A business YouTube account can be created by an individual or using a generic business account. It can then be tailored to the needs of the organization. To create a business YouTube account go to the YouTube homepage at www.youtube.com:

 Click on the Create Account link on the top menu bar

Create Account | Sign In

2   As YouTube is owned by Google, you have to have a
    Google account before you can set up your YouTube
    channel. Enter details here to create your Google account

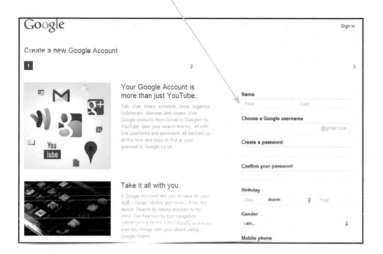

171

3   Once you have created your
    Google account you can sign
    into YouTube with your Google username and password
    by clicking on the Sign In button on the menu bar

Create Account | Sign In

4   Enter the username for your YouTube account. This will
    become part of the Web address (URL) of your channel.
    Click on the Next button

...cont'd

Editing your settings

Once you have set up your YouTube channel you can then edit your settings to create a customized look and feel. To do this:

1 Login to your account and click on the Settings button

2 Click on the Appearance button

Appearance

3 Click on the Choose File buttons to select files for the channel Avatar and Background

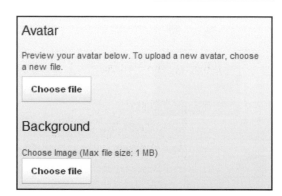

4 Click here to change the channel background

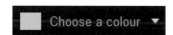

5 Click on the Info and Settings button

Info and Settings

6 Enter details about your channel including, title, description and tags for helping people find your channel

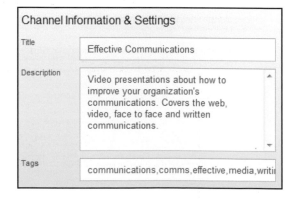

Don't forget

By default, your account username (which cannot be changed) will be the title for your channel too. However, this can be changed in the Title field in Step 6.

Uploading video

Once you have set up your YouTube channel you can start to upload and manage your video content. To do this:

1 Access your channel homepage

2 Click on the Videos button

3 Click on the Upload a Video link

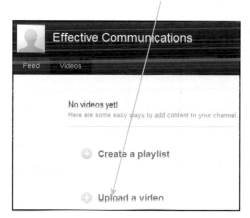

Hot tip

Video content can also be uploaded directly to YouTube from mobile devices with Internet access, such as smartphones and tablet computers.

173

4 Click on this button to upload a video file from your computer

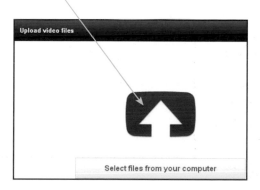

...cont'd

5 Select a video file and click on the Open button

6 The video is uploaded to your channel

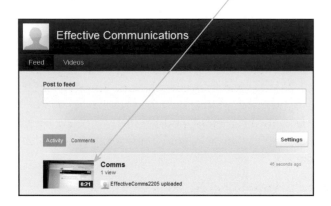

7 Click on the video to view it

8 Click on the Video Manager button to manage your video content

Embedding Video

If you want to include video on your own websites there are two main ways to do this:

- Host the video content yourself and link to it as you would with any other piece of content on your site

- Host the video on your YouTube channel and embed the code into your own site. This will create a link that plays the video on your site, by accessing it from YouTube

Publishing your own video

If you want to publish video yourself on your own website you can do this in a variety of file formats e.g. Flash, QuickTime, RealMedia, MPEG and Windows Media. These require the end user to have a suitable plug-in installed so that they can play the video format. However, most modern Web browsers contain the required plug-ins for most video. When you publish video there are two main options:

- Create a hyperlink to the video file

- Embed the video file

If you are publishing a video with a standard hyperlink the file will open in a separate window when the link is activated (as long as the user has the appropriate plug-in for the video). This is now a slightly old fashioned way of publishing video and is created with standard hyperlink HTML code: <a href="/Effective Communications/Video/Comms.MOV">

A more effective way of publishing video is to embed it into your Web page with the appropriate code. This creates a video window on your page and the user can view the video in situ on the page. When you embed video in a page it is done with the following code: <embed src="Video/Comms.MOV" width="250" height="250"></embed>

In addition to the embedded video file it is also possible to specify a range of settings for the file. These include the size of the window in which the video is displayed, a URL if you want to link to a plug-in for viewing the video and a border size for the video window.

One of the great advantages of embedding video is that it can be streamed, enabling the user to start viewing it more quickly.

Don't forget

Streaming video works by downloading the content in the background while the video is also being viewed. This is a more efficient way of publishing video for the users. It requires the video to be hosted on a video server that has streaming capability.

...cont'd

Embedding via YouTube

Another option for publishing video on your websites is to embed it within your site, but keep the video hosted on your YouTube channel. This is done with a piece of code on your own website that displays the video content on your site via YouTube. The advantages of this are:

● The video content is all hosted by YouTube so you do not have to worry about storing it

● The videos are displayed with all of the YouTube functionality so look very professional

To embed video via your YouTube channel:

Don't forget

The Share button will be available underneath any video when it is playing. However, embedding can be disabled in the Video Manager (Advanced section). If this is done then the embedding code will not be available.

1 Access one of your videos on your YouTube channel

2 Underneath the video window, click on the Share button

Share

3 The URL for the video link is displayed. Click on the Embed button

http://youtu.be/NTv5ewGfO

Embed

Options ▼

Beware

Do not publish or share any video content to which you do not have the copyright.

4 The appropriate code for embedding the video is displayed

```
<iframe width="560" height="315"
src="http://www.youtube.com/embed/NTv5ewGfOd8"
frameborder="0" allowfullscreen></iframe>
```

5 Copy the code and paste it into your own Web page. This will now display the video via your YouTube channel

11 Using Social Media

It seems that we cannot move without coming across some form of social media. This chapter shows how to use it in a business environment to best effect.

The Social Media Revolution

The biggest recent change in the world of communications has definitely been social media. The Internet has provided the means for instant, and constant, communications via sites such as Facebook, Twitter and YouTube.

Social media is an exciting and challenging area, partly because it is so immediate. Two of the crucial points to remember about social media are:

- It is not just a social tool. Used properly, it has an active role to play in the world of corporate communications

- Social media should not be used just for the sake of it. Sometimes there is a clamor to use social media for business, just because it is there and people do not want to run the risk of being left behind. However, unless there is a clear strategy for how it is to be used, this can create problems

Beware

Social media should be managed by the communications team and treated as a proper communications tool. Just because an individual spends a lot of time on Facebook or Twitter it does not necessarily mean that they are social media experts in a corporate communications arena.

Social media should not be used just for the sake of it

Social media can be a great source of good for businesses as long as it is planned and managed properly. One of the disadvantages of social media is that it is very easy to get the wrong message out into the really world. Once this is done it can spread with incredible speed via social media and it can be very, very hard to repair the damage and restore the reputation of your organization.

Because of the issues of using social media it is important to address these two points before you do anything:

- Include social media as part of your overall communications strategy (see next page)

- Create guidelines for how social media should, and should not, be used within your organization. This is essential, not so much from a disciplinary aspect for when people misuse any systems (although this should certainly be in place), but from the point of view of ensuring that no mishaps occur in the first place. It should be clearly set out about who has responsibility and administration rights for publishing content to social media sites and if necessary a review process should also be in place

A Strategy for Social Media

Although social media is a relatively new entrant to the world of corporate communications, it is one that should be treated in the same way as every other communications method.

Social media should not be used in an ad hoc manner: this is a recipe for disaster. It should be incorporated into the overall communications strategy and be used in conjunction with other communications elements.

Incorporating social media

When adding social media channels to a communications strategy some of these issues should be considered:

- Exactly what types of social media will you use? In addition to the increasingly ubiquitous Facebook and Twitter, there are also options such as wikis, blogs, online forums, podcasts and photo and video sharing sites. One point to remember is that the more elements that are included, the harder it is to manage effectively

- Will social media be used to support other channels or will it be used independently for items? Generally, it is better to use it for the former as it is more suited to providing additional information for existing communications

- The nature of social media means that it is effective as a marker for pointing towards other channels. For instance, Twitter can be used to post links to websites where there is more in-depth information

- How frequently will social media channels be updated? This may depend on what other information is being published but there should be a conscious effort to update social media as often as possible. The audience for social media expects information quickly and regularly and if you do not satisfy this then they will quickly start to look elsewhere

Using Facebook for Business

Social media sites, such as Facebook, are a very different medium from other communication channels such as paper or corporate websites and, as such, they should be treated very differently.

One of the issues with Facebook is that users have become used to it being a fun, social activity rather than associating it with business. This means that communicators have to ensure that the content of a business Facebook page is of a suitable nature to persuade users to leave their own personal pages and look at this instead. This is a considerable challenge.

Facebook content

The first thing to say about your business Facebook site is that not everyone will look at it: despite its global success, there are still a lot of people who do not use Facebook and they would certainly not think of it in a business environment. Therefore your site should not be used as the sole means of communicating important information; there are plenty of other avenues for this.

Instead, your corporate Facebook page is a much better channel for creating awareness of your organization and brand identity by include more light-hearted and fun content. A message from your CEO on your Facebook page is unlikely to entice anyone away from the thousands of more interesting things to do on social media sites.

Large corporations, such as Coca-Cola, use their Facebook sites in this way. They include stories from people from around the world about how they use the product. This creates a sense of ownership with the Facebook site while still promoting the product.

Don't forget

You can point people to your Facebook page from a link on your corporate website.

Timeline

One of the objectives of having a corporate Facebook page is to give users as much general information about your organization as possible. On websites this is usually done through an About Us section. Until recently, there was not a similar opportunity on Facebook, unless you wanted to post a lot of Status Updates of this nature.

However, with the advent of the Facebook Timeline there is now an excellent opportunity to recount your organization's history, while still giving the user the option of viewing it, or not. The Timeline was introduced in 2012 and although it was criticized initially in some quarters it has now become part of the fabric of Facebook. It works by listing all Facebook activity in chronological order. From a business perspective this is an excellent opportunity to narrate your organization's history. This can be done retrospectively so you can go back as far as you like.

181

Keeping control

When you have a corporate Facebook page anyone with the administration details can add to it. In theory this could be everyone in an organization. While this would create a very fluid, collaborative site, there is a very good reason why this should not be done. It just takes one inappropriate comment and it can be distributed around the globe in seconds.

Just as an organization would not allow anyone to update the corporate website or send out a news release, so the same controls should be in place for the Facebook site. As a general rule, the communications team should be responsible for the content on the Facebook site.

To Tweet or Not to Tweet

In 2009 an American market research company analyzed 2000 messages (tweets) on Twitter and concluded that 40% of them were 'pointless babble'. Although some viewers of Twitter may think this is a rather low figure, it does highlight one of the main issues of using Twitter in a business environment: how do you make the best use of it without it descending into mindless chitchat and 'pointless babble'?

About Twitter

Twitter is a relatively new social networking tool, launched in 2006, but it has grown at a remarkable rate and is now one of the most visited websites in the world. It is a microblogging site where users post short messages, known as tweets, of up to 140 characters. Once you have joined Twitter you can follow other users to see what they are saying and have people follow you too.

Once you have registered for Twitter, which is free, tweets can be posted from computers, smartphones and tablet computers. This makes it very quick and easy to post messages, which is one of the reasons that a lot of the messages in the Twittersphere are along the lines of, 'Just got up and had my first coffee'. This highlights one of the dangers of Twitter in a business environment: it is all too easy to post mundane messages. A good rule to follow if you are using Twitter as a business tool is:

If you don't have anything worthwhile to say, say nothing

- If you don't have anything worthwhile to say, say nothing

This does not mean that you only have to restrict yourself to dry business information. You can include humorous and light-hearted items but these should follow your Twitter strategy. This should detail:

- What to include. This should be carefully thought out. It should complement your other communication channels and every tweet should serve a purpose, even if it is just to start a conversation about a specific topic. The overall tone of tweets is also important: part of the strategy could be to only post positive or upbeat information. This creates an identity for the Twitter feed so that users know what to expect

Don't forget

One of the areas in which Twitter has come to the general public's attention has been in reporting from areas of political unrest. When there is a limited amount of information available, Twitter has become one of the main methods for local people to be able to report quickly what is actually happening.

- Who is responsible for updating your Twitter feed. In some larger organization there are dedicated teams who are responsible for managing the Twitter feed. Everyone who is involved should be given thorough training and guidelines

- Feedback. Getting ideas and feedback from customers is an excellent use of Twitter. It is a great way to respond quickly to questions and criticisms. However, if you ask for specific feedback via Twitter make sure that you frame your questions carefully and are prepared to deal with whatever comments your receive

Twitter content

As with Facebook, Twitter business content tends to focus on a 'soft' approach to promoting organizations. A lot of tweets can be classed as 'feel-good' items, not necessarily related to the organization. However, the aim of these is to encourage other users to get involved in the conversation, in the hope that they will then mention the organization and its product. This is a collaborative approach to corporate communications: creating the idea that there is a community of users out there, where the organization and its customers are all involved together.

183

Twitter functionality

There are a number of options for when you post tweets:

- Use the hashtag symbol, #, to mention other Twitter users e.g. #johnmcvey. This creates a link which users can use to visit this person's Twitter feed

- Use the at symbol, @, to add your comment to specific subjects e.g. @EffectiveComms. This is then included in the list of tweets about this topic. This is known as 'trending' with the most popular topics being flagged up on Twitter each day

- Retweeting. If you like a tweet from someone you are following you can distribute it to your followers too by retweeting it. This also becomes visible on your Twitter feed

- Adding hyperlinks. An excellent use of Twitter is to use it as a pointer to useful websites. This provides other users with additional information without using up a lot of separate tweets. Website addresses can be added by copying and pasting them into a tweet

Creating a Wiki

Wikipedia, the online encyclopedia, is another of the great successes of the dotcom era. This is a collaborative environment, where individuals can add and edit information about almost any topic. A similar tool is the wiki, a smaller version of Wikipedia where users can update websites or articles on individual topics. Its aim is to be a collaborative environment where the content is in the hands of authorized users who can update and edit it.

Wiki software

There are a number of companies who provide wiki software. Some are free, while others cost a fee. Also, they are created with different computer languages, including open source options. Some Content Management Systems also have a wiki feature built in to them. Some options to look at are:

- MediaWiki

- TikiWiki

- DocuWiki

Using Wikis

Wikis can be used to run entire websites or work on individual items. These can include:

- Creating community sites. This is where people with a shared interest can create a wiki about this

- Individual projects. Collaborating on projects in the workplace is an excellent use for a wiki. Information can be updated by each member of the project team

- Large documents such as manuals. These can sometimes be difficult to update as a lot of different people have their own ideas of what should be included and creating a lot of different versions is an issue. With a wiki, the manual can be updated and all of the interested parties can view the changes as they are being made

With a collaborative tool such as a wiki there can be some concerns about security and the accuracy of information. However, as long as everyone involved with the wiki is committed and engaged then they will ensure that any mistakes are quickly rectified and that the content is as accurate as possible.

Don't forget

As with all collaborative software, there should be clear guidelines produced about creating wikis and who has responsibility for managing them.

Online Forums

Another form of collaborative software is online forums. This is a bulletin board function where users can start conversations about different topics and then other people can add their own comments. This can cover both business and non-business topics.

As with wikis, there is a wide range of forum software on the market and this is also frequently a feature of Content Management Systems. Some options to look at are:

- phpBB
- vBulletin
- MyBB

Forums tend to offer two types of standard interaction:

- Flat. This is where each message is posted independently as part of a topic
- Threaded. This where messages can be linked into each other so that you can get a separate conversation within a topic

Moderation

One of the biggest issues of forums in a corporate environment is the posting of inappropriate material. This can be addressed with guidelines for the use of a forum, which should be as robust as possible so that everyone knows what is expected in terms of posting inappropriate content.

In addition to guidelines, forums can also be managed through moderation. This is where people are allocated to monitor the content on the forum and, if necessary, remove or edit inappropriate material. There are two main types of moderation:

- Full moderation. This is where all comments and posts have to be approved by a moderator before they are posted on the forum. This is a very resource intensive method and can act against the spontaneity of the forum
- Board moderation. This is a more realistic option for moderation and is where the moderators checks what is being posted on the forum to ensure that there is nothing inappropriate. They can also check to make sure that individuals are not being abused or bullied via the forum

Don't forget

A lot of people read messages on forums without posting anything themselves. This is known as 'lurking' and is a perfectly acceptable use of a forum.

Hot tip

Moderators can also be site administrators for a forum. This involves setting up users' permission and publishing any site-wide messages to the users.

Podcasting

As an addition to using video on your websites, podcasting is an excellent option. It is a method of creating and publishing audio files that can be broadcast on computers, MP3 players, smartphones and tablet computers.

Creating podcasts

Podcasts are created in the following way:

- The audio is recorded and edited using appropriate software. One option to try is Audacity, which is free, open source, 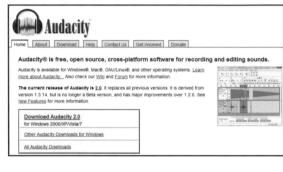 software and can be used with Windows, Mac OS X and Linux

- Output the files in a suitable format e.g. MP3, WAV or AIFF

- Publish the audio files to your website

- Once the files are published, users can listen to them on a computer or download them to an MP3 player

Uses for podcasts

Websites such as iTunes publish numerous podcasts for downloading. A lot of these are audio recordings from radio or TV shows. In a corporate environment, podcasts can be used for some of the following:

- Audio versions of video. If you use video on your websites, creating a podcast of the audio is an excellent way to distribute the information to a wider audience

- Training. This can be used to supplement classroom training and act as a refresher too

- Instructions. Podcasts can be created to explain particular methods of doing something or procedures, such as using a new, complex piece of software or equipment

Index

137

H

I

J

K

L

M

W

Y